READING 2000 • LEVEL FIVE CORE READER

Up and Away

Catherine Allan Sallie Harkness
James Love Helen McLullich
Helen Murdoch

Oliver & Boyd

Contents

Snow

One Problem After Another

The Uncertain Road

What's a Poem, Anyhow?

A Great Day

The Monday Rush

If you could lift off the roof of our house at 6.50 a.m. on a Monday you would see my mum still lying in bed and you would hear her mutter, "I wish that there were two Saturdays a week."

AMANDA DEAN, 9

Mother and father have overslept.
The dog has got mother's shoe.
Father yells with pain as the cat digs her claws into the sole of his foot.
Children race about, it's ten past eight.
Shoes have to be cleaned.
Buttons need sewing on.
The breakfast needs cooking.
School books have to be found and put into satchels.
Help! The toaster is on fire.
Money for dinners has to be dug out of father's trouser pocket.
Quick, where are the car keys?
Oh dear, the back door is not locked.
There are the car keys on the sideboard.
Off goes the car.
Help! Mother has left her shopping basket behind.
At last they are off, half an hour late.

NICOLA TOOSEY, 12

You're Late...

Mouse came slowly down the stairs in the morning. There was a small round hole in the plaster by the front door, and Mouse had once drawn an arrow to the hole and had written DROP COINS HERE BEFORE EXITING. He went out the door, looking down at his feet, taking the steps one at a time. He was trying to be late for school now that his efforts not to go at all had failed.

"Mom, I'm sick, hear? I'm really sick," he had said at breakfast. He had been sick too. "I can't even eat, I'm so sick."

"All right, if you're sick, show me some fever," his mother had said, getting up from the table and going into the bathroom for the thermometer. "If you don't have a fever, you aren't sick enough to stay home."

He had sat at the table while she went for the thermometer, thinking of how much he missed his father. Breakfast had been a different meal before his father started driving a truck.

His mother returned with the thermometer and he said, "There are lots of illnesses that you don't have a fever with, Mom. Didn't you ever hear of food poisoning?"

"Put this in your mouth."

He had known it was hopeless, but he had kept the thermometer in his mouth, rubbing it with his tongue just in case the friction might somehow cause the mercury to rise.

His mother waited by the table. Then she removed the

thermometer and looked at it.

"Normal. Get your books and go to school."

"Mom, I am *sick*."

"Go."

Slowly Mouse left the apartment and walked in the direction of school. He knew he would have to be very late in order to miss Marv Hammerman, because Hammerman never went into school until the last possible minute. He just lounged outside with his friends.

The street was empty except for two ladies talking, and Garbage Dog who was standing by the ladies looking up at them. There was the faint aroma of bacon grease about one of the ladies.

"Go on," one of the ladies said, kicking at him.

Garbage Dog moved back a few steps and continued to stand watching them. On his short legs he appeared to be lying down. Mouse remembered that he had once measured Garbage Dog's legs as part of an arithmetic assignment about learning to use the ruler. Each student had had to measure ten things, and the first thing Mouse had measured was Garbage Dog's legs. They were not quite three inches long.

It had been an impressive way to start out the list of things he had measured. Garbage Dog's legs – two and seven-eighths inches.

At least half the people in the class had not believed that figure.

"Hey, no dog's got legs that short," one boy had cried.

"This one does."

"Two and seven-eighths inches?"

"Yes, two and seven-eighths inches."

"That's just *that* long."

"I know. Listen, I can bring this dog to class if you want me to, Miss Regent. I can catch him and we can – "

"No, Benjie," Miss Regent had said quickly, "I don't think that will be necessary. Some dogs do have very short legs."

"But two and seven-eighths inches!" the boy had cried again, holding up his paper ruler. "That's just *that* long."

Mouse knelt and scratched Garbage Dog behind the ears. He must have hit the spot where it really itched, because Garbage Dog leaned back, his nose pointing to the sky, and started making a moaning noise.

"That feel good?" It was surprising, Mouse thought, that a dog like this who had never known soap or flea powder could smell so nice and fresh. It was a kind of dairy and dry leaves smell. "There? Is that where it itches?"

The quiet of the street made Mouse think he was late enough.

"I better go."

Still kneeling, he took out his pencil, wrote SCRATCH ME on a smooth spot on the sidewalk and drew a little arrow to Garbage Dog. Then he rose.

As he walked, Hammerman came back into his mind. It seemed to Mouse that everything, everybody, had suddenly shrunk in importance, making Marv Hammerman a giant. Hammerman towered over the street in Mouse's mind so that the buildings were toys around his ankles, and the pigeons that roosted on the roofs flew around Hammerman's knees.

Mouse walked slower and when he got to the school, it was deserted. The late bell was ringing. Mouse took the steps two at a time and then ran down the hall to his room.

"You're late, Benjie," Mr Stein said, looking up at Mouse from his desk.

"Yes, Sir, my mom thought I was sick."

From *The Eighteenth Emergency* by BETSY BYARS

I've Got an Apple Ready

My hair's tightly plaited;
I've a bright blue bow;
I don't want my breakfast,
And now I must go.

My satchel's on my shoulder;
Nothing's out of place;
And I've got an apple ready,
Just in case.

So it's 'Goodbye, Mother!'
And off down the street;
Briskly at first
On pit-a-pat feet,

But slow and more slow
As I reach the tarred
Trackway that runs
By Hodson's yard;

For it's there sometimes
Bill Craddock waits for me
To snatch off my beret
And throw it in a tree.

Bill Craddock leaning
On Hodson's rails;
Bill with thin hands
And dirty nails;

Bill with a front tooth
Broken and bad;
His dark eyes cruel,
And somehow sad.

Often there are workmen,
And then he doesn't dare;
But this morning I feel
He'll be there.

At the corner he will pounce ...
But quickly I'll say,
"Hallo, Bill, have an apple!" –
In an ordinary way.

I'll push it in his hand
And walk right on;
And when I'm round the corner
I'll run!

JOHN WALSH

Believe it or not!

Every few years or so the subject of UFOs – Unidentified Flying Objects – creates a lot of general public interest when yet another story of strange objects having been seen in the sky is reported by a newspaper or on television.

Sometimes such reports give rise to heated debates as 'experts' are called upon to give their opinions on what they think has been seen. It is at this point, you can be sure, that the subject will be extended to include theories about alien space ships, flying saucers and 'Close Encounters of the Third Kind'!

Before long the original 'sighting' which started the debate will have been forgotten and all sorts of possible and impossible explanations for UFOs in general will have been offered and no satisfactory conclusions reached!

Believe it or not, this is just what happened on 18 January 1979 in the House of Lords, the Upper House of the British Parliament. That evening, at seven minutes past seven, the Earl of Clancarty rose to begin the debate. The subject on the order paper was UFOs – Unidentified Flying Objects.

The timing of the debate was faultless. All over Britain, strange lights had been seen in the sky on New Year's Eve, and some eye-witnesses had described a flaming spacecraft, complete with brightly-lit portholes, flying eerily over the snowy winter landscape.

In Italy, UFO sightings had reached epidemic proportions, with newspapers and television headlining the report by naval officers of a 275m-long fiery craft rising out of the Adriatic, and the photograph of a UFO taken by a policeman in Palermo.

On the other side of the world, in New Zealand, a shaken television reporter and his film crew described a terrifying night flight alongside a UFO. Only hours later, the air-waves of the world were alive with their remarkable film of the event.

Lord Clancarty, author of several books on UFOs, opened the debate. He had certain requests to make of the British Government. First, he wished it to prepare its citizens for the coming of UFOs, and to allay the fears of many people that the Government was in league with the United States to 'cover up' the truth about Unidentified Flying Objects.

Secondly, Lord Clancarty called on the authorities to press for a worldwide study of UFOs so that the results could be passed on to the public.

Finally, he wanted the Minister of

Defence to appear on television to discuss the British Government's own assessment of UFOs.

Lord Clancarty's main argument was that it is impossible to doubt the existence of UFOs because they had been seen by so many sincere and ordinary people. In addition, many trained observers such as pilots, coastguards, police officers and radar operators had also seen them.

Many of the reported sightings of UFOs could not be explained and therefore should be fully investigated by responsible government authorities. Lord Clancarty and his supporters believed that UFOs were extra-terrestrial craft which were spying on the earth. They had a strong case – no one had yet been able to prove otherwise!

Lord Strabolgi, who spoke on behalf of the Government, was not impressed by the arguments which Lord Clancarty and his supporters had put forward. Although it was not possible to provide a satisfactory explanation for *all* reported sightings of UFOs, there was no proof that the strange objects which had been seen were 'alien spacecraft'!

In fact, almost anything that flies in the sky had been mistaken, at one time or another, for a UFO – migrating birds and insects, clouds, aircraft landing lights, comets, meteors and planets. Indeed, the planet Venus had been mistaken so often for some sort of spacecraft that it had earned the title of 'the Queen of the UFOs'.

Lord Strabolgi bluntly stated the position as he and his colleagues saw it. "There is nothing to convince the Government that there has ever been a single visit by an alien spacecraft, let alone the number of visits which the noble earl, Lord Clancarty, claims are increasing all the time. There really are tens of thousands of strange things to be seen. It is the custom to call such phenomena 'UFOs', and to translate this into 'alien spacecraft'. All we can say is that there is a great variety of plain explanations."

Lord Strabolgi was also at pains to emphasise that there was not, and never had been, a 'cover up' of the truth by the British Government. UFO reports were studied to see if they contained anything of interest to the Ministry of Defence. These reports were kept confidential only to protect the identities of the people who made them. Lord Strabolgi, on behalf of the British Government, rejected Lord Clancarty's plea for an investigation into UFOs.

And so, at the end of the debate, which had lasted for three hours, little more had been achieved than an airing of views. Neither side had been able to convince the other. However, it would be surprising if, as they left the Houses of Parliament on that January night, each of those who took part had not glanced up into the sky and wondered.

Adapted from *Arthur C. Clarke's Mysterious World*
by SIMON WELFARE AND JOHN FARLEY

Brief Encounter

And then in my dreams I slipped away
To the silver ship in the dawn of day,
To the grasshopper men with their queer green eyes
And suits that glittered in splendid dyes.
They came, they said, from a thirsty land,
A land that was dead and choked with sand;
The wells were empty and dusty and dry,
And the burning sun hung low in the sky;
"We are old," they said. "We have had our day,
And the silent cities crumble away."
"Yet here," they said, "we may find again
All that was carefree and lovely then
When the wells were full and the cities rang
With the harvest song that the reapers sang!"

ANON.

The Marrog

My desk's at the back of the class
  And nobody, nobody knows
    I'm a Marrog from Mars
With a body of brass
  And seventeen fingers and toes.

Wouldn't they shriek if they knew
  I've three eyes at the back of my head
    And my hair is bright purple
My nose is deep blue
  And my teeth are half-yellow, half-red.

My five arms are silver, and spiked
  With knives on them sharper than spears.
I could go back right now, if I liked –
  And return in a million light years.

I could gobble them all,
For I'm seven foot tall
  And I'm breathing green flames from my ears.

Wouldn't they yell if they knew,
  If they guessed that a Marrog was here?
Ha-ha, they haven't a clue –
  Or wouldn't they tremble with fear!
"Look, look, a Marrog!"
  They'd all scream – and SMACK
The blackboard would fall and the ceiling would crack
  And teacher would faint, I suppose.
But I grin to myself, sitting right at the back
  And nobody, nobody knows.

R.C. Scriven

Up and Away

A few long minutes went by and then a dim shape came out of the shadows and crossed the road. Jonk and Bill went to meet him, the soft soles of their shoes crackling faintly on the sparkling pavement. It was freezing hard.

"You managed it then." Even out in the road Bill kept his voice low.

Jonk thought how pale and thin Arf seemed but, while she and Bill shivered as they sniffed the air, he had not even bothered to turn up his jacket collar.

"I turned the electricity off at the mains," he said.

"They think it's a power cut."

Bill laughed.

"Come on." Jonk was impatient to get on with their plan.

They went to the corner and looked round. Policemen might be the biggest danger at this stage of their journey, but all was clear. They trotted up the centre of the road. The little black bags were already resting snugly between their shoulders but they had decided only to take off when there was no chance of being seen.

They paused at the next corner. Nobody in sight, but before they ran off they glanced back.

They saw it simultaneously. In the centre of the road a hundred yards behind them, watching them as its breath steamed around its head, stood the black dog.

"Run!" said Bill.

They were heading for the park, and it was still some streets away. More than one person, sleeping lightly, heard the quick but furtive sound of running feet and a second or two later the sound of a dog's feet as it streaked behind them.

They turned two corners and reached a third.

"Stop!" Bill ordered.

The dog rounded the corner behind them, moving fast. Bill held their arms and stopped them running. The dog saw them and halted. "It's not trying to catch us."

They and the dog regarded each other, the length of the street between. Their tension eased slightly but then another danger stiffened their muscles. In a street to their left a patrolling policeman crossed the road to try the door of a corner shop. Their route lay to the right, but if they ran now they would attract his attention.

"Walk to the next corner," Bill said.

They stayed on the pavement, often looking back at the double danger behind them, but the policeman walked on sedately, and the dog was content merely to keep them in sight. They planned their next move.

"We mustn't let it see us go up," said Jonk.

"Why not?" Even now, Arf challenged her, but it was Bill who answered.

"Because its master might see what it sees," he said.

Arf looked sideways at him but said nothing.

At the next corner they turned right, and ahead of them they could see the trees of the park. Without a word they broke into a run. At the end of the road they crossed to where the wire fence and tall hedge enclosing the park followed the line of the road. They ran fast for a hole in the fence. Jonk and Arf were through, but Bill was still outside when the dog rounded the corner.

"No use," he said. "It's seen me."

He pushed through to join them.

"Now we try phase two," he said.

They moved out over the grass. The sky was bright and clear above. They had all the space they needed. It would have been a perfect place to take off and Arf wanted to risk it, put Jonk turned a furious face on him.

"No!" she said. "We'll do what we said."

Bill glanced back. The dog was behaving exactly as they hoped.

"Good dog," Bill murmured. Then he turned to the others. "Ready?" he said. "Just a few more yards."

They were approaching the bowling green that was ringed by trees. On the side of the green nearest them was the pavilion. Once again Bill looked back.

"Dog's coming," he said. "Get ready."

They reached behind their heads and grasped the loops between their shoulders but did not pull. They walked on.

"One," said Bill, counting their steps.

"Two. Three. Go!"

They ran. Four steps took them level with the pavilion. Two more put it between them and the dog. They jumped the little ditch on to the green and fanned out. Together they pulled the loops.

They had not previously tried to take off running. It was a new sensation. Before their arms were fully extended, their feet were only lightly touching the ground. A split second later they were clear, drifting over the green. They took great bites of air with their arms and rose swiftly.

The dog hurtled round the corner of the pavilion, low to the ground and scattering stones as it hit the ditch. They were twenty feet above it. They saw it casting around for their scent before the trees hid it. As they crossed the park boundary, gaining height over the rooftops, they heard its wolf howl searching the shadows below.

They climbed until the roofs of the city lay beneath them like a crumpled carpet patterned by rows of lights. They swam over it, peering down, but they could see nothing moving in the black square of the park.

They flew towards the outskirts, moving gingerly

through the icy air in case some barrier extended upwards from the city wall to keep them in, but their toes trailed past the fringes of the lights and they were outside.

They breathed easier and went forward at speed, searching the ground for the road that led to the backlands. But the earth below was dark, a jumble of shadows with, here and there, a silver glint of the moon on water.

Arf could not use his compass, and they slowed – winnowing with their hands to keep height as they searched for a landmark.

"We'll get lost," said Bill. "Let's go down and look at the map."

They sank towards a field, going down into it suspiciously, feeling, as they got below tree height, that they were being swallowed. Their feet pressed into the frozen grass. The night was absolutely still.

"Cold up there," said Bill.

Under the moon the frost was a powdery grey, but in spite of it the earth seemed to give them warmth. They rubbed their hands and arms and then crouched close to shield the light of the torch as they examined the map. They could not be sure where they were but they tried to memorise some of the roads and they took a compass bearing. Then they climbed towards the sky.

The landscape was vague and they were wandering uncertainly in the general direction of the backlands when a lorry came from the city and drew a line for them with its headlights along the road they wanted. It soon turned off, but they could see enough to travel fast.

The road was often hidden, sometimes seeming to be squeezed out of existence by the fields, and often impossible to distinguish from hedgerows, but they were always able to pick up its dark band ahead or follow its hidden track by the houses which dotted it like knots in a piece of string.

They flew in line abreast, only a few feet separating their finger-tips. The cold air bit their throats, but even though they did not have to make huge strokes with their arms to move at speed, it was enough to keep them warm.

From *The Giant under the Snow* by JOHN GORDON

Night Flying

The world turns:
so turn I.
The moon rises:
so rise I.
All night long the stars and I
wheel to the wing tips,
lean to the west.
Darkness inhabits me,
dreams wash over me;
down to the land
the houses lie cosily
the rocks crouch tightly,
shadows creep noisily,
and far to the south
the river runs brightly.
So the world turns:
so turn I.
The moon rises:
so rise I.

MOYRA CALDECOTT

Labels

"I thank God I was evacuated: not because I avoided danger, which was the purpose of evacuation, but because it changed my way of thinking. It made me love the country ....

When I look back on those days I know I found a refuge, quiet and peaceful: I found another family whom I really loved, and still do."

MAY OWEN

"I have this image of a small boy with a label tied round his neck. The boy has no features and is crying.

He is carrying a cardboard box, which contains his gasmask ....

Even nowadays whenever I travel anywhere and have to say goodbye to my own children, I identify with that small boy. I remember the label and the gasmask and the anxiety. I write my name on the luggage labels and hope I do not return to find my home bombed to ruins and my identity lost somewhere underneath the rubble."

MEL CALMAN

Soon, no one will care to remember
your blackout nights
your blackened lives
and charred childhoods

I wish I could always be thankful
that I will never see
a night sky of barrage balloons and searchlights

R. EMMERSON

Evacuation

In the four days ending Monday, 4 September 1939 the British Government's plan for the evacuation of children in the event of war was put into operation. During this period over one and a half million people, school pupils and their teachers and mothers with young families, were

transported by road, rail and even sea to areas which were considered to be comparatively safe. It was thought that the declaration of war would be followed immediately by the large scale bombing from the air of cities, large towns, dockyards and industrial centres.

The Civil Defence Bill of July 1939 provided that any additional expense caused by evacuation would be repaid to local authorities by the Exchequer. It also gave compulsory billeting powers which allowed local authorities to demand accommodation for evacuees from householders in 'safe' reception areas. A scale of allowance was drawn up and the extent to which evacuees should be fed and looked after was defined in the Bill.

During the weeks that followed the declaration of war on 3 September, thousands more children were moved from the cities as their parents took advantage of the opportunity to send them away from danger to be cared for by foster-parents. However, not all parents agreed that their children should be sent away and many of those who did, changed their minds when the bombing of the cities did not begin as expected. Some children remained with their foster-parents for the duration of the war while others returned home – only to be sent away again when the air raids began.

This movement of evacuees to and from the reception areas continued throughout the war years.

Away from it all

It was late August. The sun shone as never before and the weather prospects looked good for the remaining week of our holiday.

We rowed across the bay to the White Shore to swim in the cool, calm waters of the loch. As we lazed in the warm sunshine, watching the yachts slide in to the harbour to replenish supplies or anchor for the night, vague thoughts of war haunted us, making an uneasy intrusion upon the tranquillity that surrounded us.

Newspaper headlines struck a note of stark reality.

Thursday 24th August ....

GOVERNMENT TO ASK FOR EMERGENCY POWERS

It all seemed so remote from the peaceful summer day.

But that evening, as we gathered round the wireless, an ugly cloud suddenly cast its dark shadow over us as we listened to the grim warning.

> "Here is a special announcement.
>
> In view of the present situation, the Ministry of Health issues the following warning:
>
> It is desirable that teachers from schools in the evacuating areas should return to duty and report at their schools on the morning of Saturday, 26 August.
>
> The Government wishes to emphasise that this is *not* a notification that evacuation is to take place.
>
> If evacuation should become necessary, full notice will be given and everyone concerned will be told what to do.
>
> The possibility of putting an evacuation scheme for school children into operation depends, as is well known, on organisation by school units under the charge of their teachers. Teachers are key-men and their attendance at their posts, like that of other key-men, is important under the present circumstances."

In silence we packed up our holiday luggage to be ready for an early morning start and wondered, sadly, when and if we should see each other again.

On the morning of 26 August I reported to the east-end city school where I taught. All but one of the staff were present as the headmaster briefed us on plans for the evacuation and advised us that, for such a major operation, a rehearsal would be necessary.

On the following Monday the rehearsal went ahead without a hitch, and staff and pupils were asked to report next day for normal classes. Normal classes? The undercurrent of excitement and uncertainty made concentration impossible and it seemed as if the school day would never end.

Newspaper headlines continued to depress.

Wednesday 30th August ....
PEACE OR WAR
Issues still undecided
Thursday 31st August ....
CRISIS NEARING ITS CLIMAX
Friday 1st September ....
LAST EFFORTS FOR PEACE

Although there were no classes on Saturday, we were asked to report at 9 a.m. on 2 September. When we did we found a notice posted on the school gate.

Evacuation would take place.

We were instructed to assemble in the school playground at 7 o'clock the following morning. We were to take the minimum of luggage and some food for the journey. Each person must carry the gasmask that had already been supplied.

In a strange sort of way it came as a relief that the waiting was almost over.

On Sunday morning we straggled along the route we had rehearsed barely a week before. At the railway station our train was already waiting for us. There were tearful goodbyes as parents hugged their children and waved sadly until the last carriage disappeared from view, heading for an unknown destination.

Travelling by train was a novelty for most of the children and as they ate their way through the morning, the atmosphere in the compartment was more like that of a school outing. There were many stops on the way, for we were frequently shunted into sidings while more urgent transport rattled along the main line. After seven hours we had still not reached our destination.

At 3.30 p.m. we pulled into a large station, the name of which had been covered over as had those of all the stations we had passed through. I wound down the window, hoping that we had arrived at last.

Not only was I disappointed to find that we had still further to travel, but I learned from a porter that war had been declared!

HELEN MCLULLICH

Evacuees

Four years ago
They came to this little town
Carrying their bundles – women who did not know
Where the sky would lie when their babies were born, mothers
With children, children with sisters and brothers,
Children with schoolmates, and frightened children alone.
They saw the strangers at the station, the sea-mist on the hill,
In the windless waiting days when the walls of Poland fell.

NORMAN NICHOLSON

An End and a Beginning

"The full meaning of what it meant to be an evacuee only became clear to me at the final moment of departure. We had been labelled, washed, brushed, kissed and clouted when we howled for mothers, fathers, brothers and lost toys. And here we suddenly were, crammed by the dozen into dingy railway carriages, rolling down the line towards the west of Wales, with a chorus of women wailing in our equally tearful wake.

I was a small shabby boy, suddenly motherless and brotherless, lost in a trainful of other howling strangers.

One childhood was over and another beginning."

BRYNN GRIFFITHS

Two Willows, One Sandwich

She ticked them off on her list, saying aloud, "Two Willows, one Sandwich."

Nick clung to Carrie's sleeve as they went through the door into a long, dark room with pointed windows. It was crowded and noisy.

Someone said to Carrie, "Would you like a cup of tea, bach? And a bit of cake, now?" She was a cheerful, plump woman with a sing-song voice. Carrie shook her head; she felt cake would choke her.

"Stand by there, then," the woman said. "There by the wall with the others, and someone will choose you."

Carrie looked round, bewildered, and saw Albert Sandwich. She whispered, "What's happening?" and he answered, "A kind of cattle auction, it seems."

He sounded calmly disgusted. He gave Carrie her suitcase, then marched to the end of the hall, sat down on his own, and took a book out of his pocket.

Carrie wished she could do that. Sit down and read as if nothing else mattered. But she had already begun to feel ill with shame at the fear that no one would choose her, the way she always felt when they picked teams at school. Suppose she was left to the last! She dragged Nick into the line of waiting children and stood, eyes on the ground, hardly daring to breathe. When someone called out, "A nice little girl for Mrs Davies, now," she felt she would suffocate. She looked up but unfocused her eyes so that passing faces blurred and swam in front of her.

Nick's hand tightened in hers. She looked at his white

face and the traces of sick round his mouth and wanted to shake him. No one would take home a boy who looked like that, so pale and delicate. They would think he was bound to get ill or be a trouble to them. She said in a low, fierce voice, "Why don't you smile and look nice?" and he blinked with surprise, looking so small and so sweet that she softened. She said,

"Oh, it's all right, I'm not cross. I won't leave you."

Minutes passed, feeling like hours. Children left the line and were taken away. Only unwanted ones were left, Carrie thought. She and Nick, and a few tough-looking boys, and an ugly girl with a squint who had two little sisters. And Albert Sandwich who was still sitting quietly on his suitcase, reading his book and taking no notice. *He* didn't care! Carrie tossed her head and hummed under her breath to show she didn't either.

Someone had stopped in front of her. Someone said, "Surely you can take two, Miss Evans?"

"Two girls, perhaps. Not a boy and a girl, I'm afraid. I've only the one room, see, and my brother's particular."

Particular about what, Carrie wondered. But Miss Evans looked nice; a little like a red squirrel Carrie had once seen, peering round a tree in a park. Reddish brown hair and bright, button eyes, and a shy, quivering look.

Carrie said, "Nick sleeps in my room at home because he has bad dreams sometimes. I always look after him and he's no trouble at all."

Miss Evans looked doubtful. "Well, I don't know what my brother will say. Perhaps I can chance it." She smiled at Carrie. "There's pretty eyes you have, girl! Like green glass!"

Carrie smiled back. People didn't often notice her when Nick was around. *His* eyes were dark blue, like their mother's. She said, "Oh, Nick's the pretty one, really."

From *Carrie's War*
by NINA BAWDEN

Cold Comfort

John came out of the grocer's shop, and stood a moment on the corner of the street. He stopped to put the ration books in the pocket of his blazer, and to arrange the brown paper bag with three eggs in it carefully on top of his basket. While he stood there the children came streaming out of the school on the other side of the street. First came a dark-haired, scruffy-looking boy in big boots, and after him trooped a whole crowd of yelling boys, among whom John recognised the local bullies.

As soon as the group turned the corner and were out of sight of the school gates, the yelling changed to a raucous sing-song chant.

"Ya, lousy Londoner! Ya, lousy Londoner!" The scruffy boy walked on, not quickening his pace, not turning his head.

"Look out!" screamed a jeering voice. "There's a bomb coming!"

"Run for a coal-hole, quick!" suggested another.

"Go and live in Scotland – no bombs there!" cried another voice.

"That's right. We don't want you here, you and your stinking lice!" chorused the rest.

The boy was walking past John now. His face was very stiff, the lips pressed close together. John put down the shopping basket, and stepped behind him, across the path of his pursuers.

"Stop that!" he ordered firmly.

They stopped in their tracks. Then a curious shuffling movement started among them, as the front row sidled sideways, until a space was opened down the middle of the group, and the ringleader, who appeared to lead his gang from the back, stood facing John.

"Stop what?" he said, glancing round him. It was no place for a fight. Only a little way down the road was a bus queue, shoppers were passing them, and a policeman would be along in seconds if they started trouble. And any minute the teachers would finish staffroom tea, and come round the corner on their way to catch buses home.

"I mean leave him alone. He can't help being an evacuee. So shut up."

"I don't care whether he can help it," said the boy deliberately. "I don't like him. He stinks. Of slums."

John flushed. "You ought to be ashamed of yourself!" he said. "Your father, and my father, are fighting, or risking their lives to keep this a free country, and you go picking on someone for what they can't help, like any beastly Nazi!"

There was a pause. Then John turned on his heel, and found the scruffy boy still standing just behind him, watching.

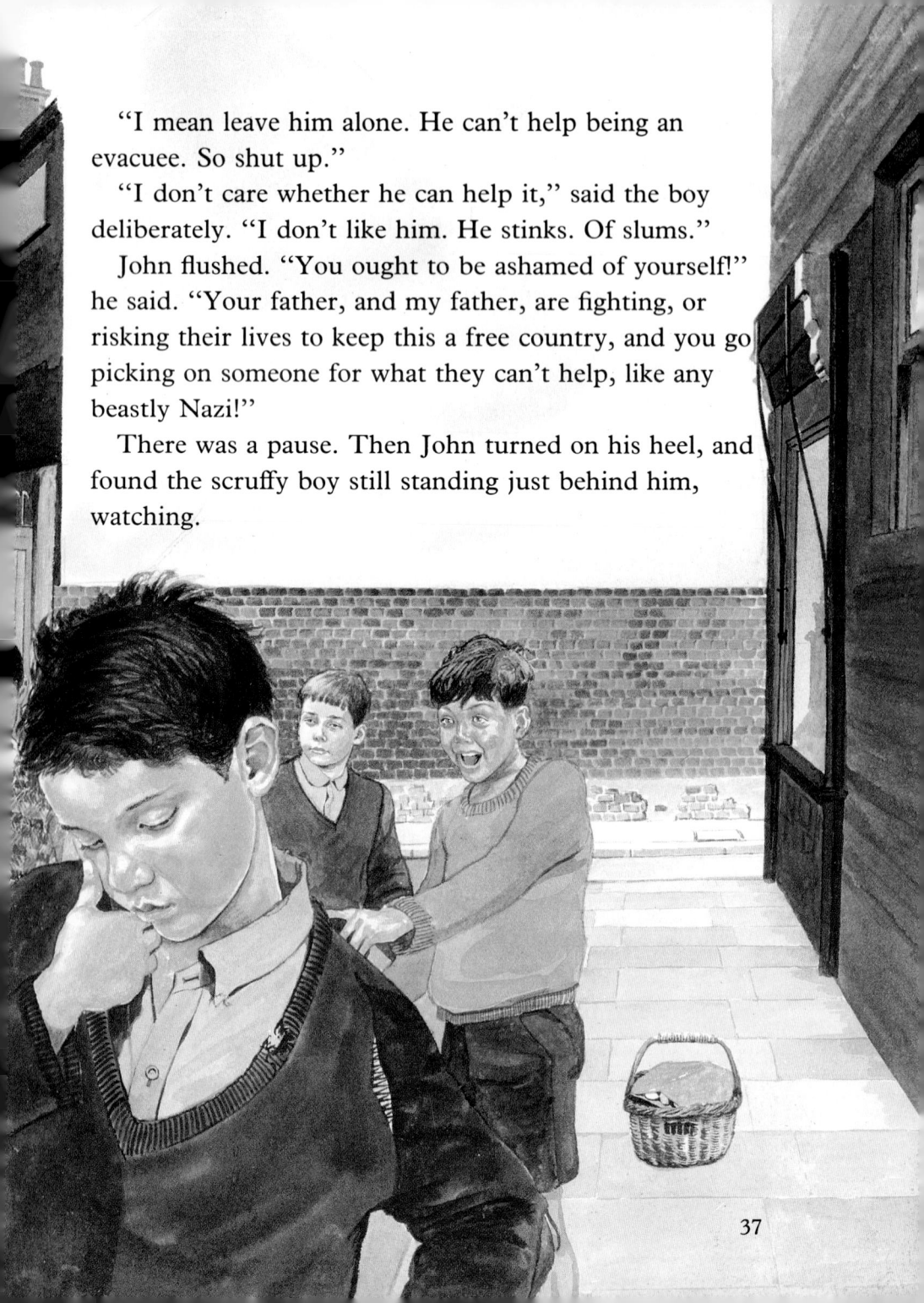

"Come on," said John to him, and they walked away down the street. This might have been a dignified way of going, had John not forgotten the shopping basket, but he had gone only a few paces when he had to turn round and run hastily back for it. There was a roar of laughter from the gang, and the rude yells began again behind their backs.

"Get on your high horse about your dad, don't you? What about your brother?"

"Ya, dirty conchie!"

"Dirty yellow conchie!" This time it was John who walked steadily with his face set like a stone. But the ordeal did not last long; the gang did not follow them. They walked along together in silence for some way. There was nothing in particular to talk about. They passed a large poster which said,

Your Courage
Your Cheerfulness
Your Resolution
Will Bring *Us* Victory

but all the rude remarks this suggested were old jokes now.

They passed a newsagent's and John went in to buy an evening paper; his mother liked to see the news. The paper was full of the fighting in Norway. John expected the scruffy boy to walk on, but he was waiting when John came out of the shop.

"Is he going to thank me? I do hope not," thought

John uneasily. But out of the corner of his eye he just caught a glimpse of a boy slinking back into a doorway a little way down the street. The gang had not given up after all.

"I'll walk home with you," he said to the boy.

"Don't bother – they only yell. All bite and no bark like."

"Well they don't do either while we keep together. I'll come."

The boy put on an odd, swaggering, couldn't-care-less expression. "Please yourself," he said.

They turned up a side road. There were only a few houses along it, and then it turned into a track across a field to Hunter's Farm, the other side of the railway. But they walked past all the houses, and came to the gate into the field.

"I'm all right from here. Thanks a lot, mate," said the boy.

"I'm John – John Aston."

"Oh, I'm Pat Riley. Thanks for the walk."

"Where are you going? I didn't know there were any evacuees at Hunter's Farm."

Again an odd expression flickered across Pat's face.

"In this here field," he declared, "there's accommodation for a small herd of cows and an evacuee family. The farmer says will the family please mind not to disturb the cows. But he can't tell his blasted cows not to frighten my mum!"

From *The Dolphin Crossing*
by Jill Paton Walsh

A Warm Smile

I was the only child left in the school after the sorting. All the other kids had been taken by their people. It had been like a market for children, sorting them out, looking them over. There were a few tears as we parted from our friends, but we promised to meet again the following day. Apparently my lady hadn't arrived. Someone said, in my hearing, "I'll take her if she doesn't come." I felt like a scrag end. But the door burst open and in she came, a golden-haired, beautifully-dressed lady with the most gorgeous smile. "Is this my little girl?" she said. I prayed, yes please! and it was my lady come for me at last.

"Come along *home*, May, you must be tired, but I want you to meet my mother and sister Enid who will be

longing to meet you," she said. And home it was to me in every sense of the word.

Myrtle Cottage was out of this world for me, full of lovely things, with a wonderful garden, an orchard and a car, too. Most wonderful of all, Miss Eilean's sister Enid bred bull terriers, and there were lots of them in the orchard in kennels.

At first I felt very shy as I realised what sort of a home I had come to: gentry we used to call these people, very well educated, spoke posh, had always been used to the best in life. Here was I, a cockney kid born by the docks in the East End of London and used to nothing but poverty. The contrast was enormous. But never by word or deed was I in any way made to feel different.

Mrs Alexander was the most gracious of ladies. I used to love walking to church on Sundays with her. I was never made to do any jobs, as a lady came in to 'do', but I always kept my room clean and so on and liked to wash up and help, because everyone was so full of praise. I would have done anything for any one of them.

I grew to love Allerford and district even more in the coming weeks. I had never felt such peace, it was a refuge for me. I had a happy home life, new friends made in the village, and there was so much to do: whist drives, meetings, church activities, and I was even picked for the choir.

My life was so completely full and happy, and so different, I never realised a war was on.

MAY OWEN

The Rough with the Smooth

The tall woman and I stared at each other. I saw that her hair was white, streaked with grey. She wore glasses which rested on a generous nose. I stared up two large, round nostrils. Her eyes were fierce, but her mouth was wide and smiling. She wore a cotton dress with flowers on it, an apron over this with more flowers, thick brown wrinkly stockings and black shoes which bulged painfully in several places.

What she saw was, I suppose, a round-faced little boy with spiky hair and dark rings under his eyes; travel-stained shirt, Fair Isle pullover, short trousers above thin legs, scuffed shoes. And a label.

I was the first to speak – and what I said would have made Dickens proud.

"Please, I'm the new evacuee," I said.

Strange that I don't remember what she said, but I know that she led me into the kitchen and sat me at the table. I kept the same position at that table for the next four and a half years.

I don't know how Rose Larcombe would have rated as a cook; small boys judge by quantity, and a poor cook would be someone who gave you an excess of Brussels sprouts. Two features of Aunt Rose's meals were to become familiar. First, her new potatoes. They were the smallest, sweetest things imaginable. She made a good gravy, and when those delicious pebbles were sliced open and splashed around, ecstasy wasn't far off. Unfortunately it wasn't long-lived either; because no matter what we

had for 'afters' Aunt Rose insisted that I took bread with it. Every mouthful of prunes, or rice-pudding, or just plain custard, had to be followed by the hateful bread and marge. Why she made this rule still baffles me. Perhaps she reasoned that if I ate more bread, I'd eat less of the other stuff, and so supplies would last longer; she may honestly have thought that it was good for me; or it may have been a local custom. Or it could be that it was intended to be an early lesson in life: that too much undiluted pleasure is bad for the soul, one must take the rough with the smooth and so on.

MICHAEL ASPEL

Pot Luck

The idea of becoming a substitute parent to a complete stranger could not have been a happy prospect for many of those who provided a home for an evacuee. Yet many did so, for various reasons.

Some may have seen it as a patriotic duty – their contribution to the war effort; a way to demonstrate their willingness to do their bit 'for king and country'.

Many may have had little choice. A visit from a billeting officer, a hurried inspection of available accommodation, a brief explanation of official requirements and allowances, a name ticked off on a form, and suddenly an unexpected addition to the family was a possibility.

BETTER POT-LUCK
with Churchill today
THAN HUMBLE PIE
under Hitler tomorrow
DON'T WASTE FOOD!

Another kind of pot luck! During the Second Worl War the Ministry of Foo issued posters like these t

Others, no doubt, welcomed the opportunity to provide refuge from danger for a child suddenly uprooted from home, family and friends.

Whatever the reasons, the moment of truth for some came when a nervous, homesick, travel-weary bundle (like a badly wrapped, but neatly labelled, parcel) arrived at the front door. The thoughts of both adult and child must have been pretty much the same: What now? What do I say? Will she like me? Will I like her?

It was all a matter of pot luck. For some it worked. For others it didn't. No matter how well-prepared a foster-mum might have been, or how willing the child was, it was not easy to build up a quick, comfortable relationship.

It is remarkable that so many were able to do so and to turn what could have been simply 'board and lodging' into 'home from home'.

Your own vegetables
all the year round...
if you
DIG FOR
VICTORY NOW

how people how they ould contribute to the ar effort by saving and rowing their own food.

The Return

I was four years old when the war began. When they loaded us into buses and took us off to the station I was too young to realise what was happening.

Thinking back on it now, with my own son nearly four years old, I wonder how our parents were able to let us go. In similar circumstances, I sometimes ask myself, would my wife and I tie a label on our son's lapel and send him off to an unknown destination, to be looked after by strangers for five of the most important years of his life?

★ ★ ★ ★ ★ ★

Not only do I have few memories of the years I spent in Devon, but some of those I do have are not ones I would have expected to retain. I find it difficult to understand why I remember so clearly the coloured erasers in the shop window. I was convinced that a blue eraser was for rubbing out blue pencil marks, and so on. Why does this trivial memory stay, when I have no memories at all of changing from one family to another? I even changed town, moving to nearby Paignton, but I have no memories of this, or the other moves.

Instead I remember having German measles, and being bitten by a dog, feeling proud of a new overcoat, going for walks through country lanes. I remember my father visiting me, and my grandfather coming to fetch me home. No other impressions remain, though I search for them as a miser seeks for his lost gold.

The journey home with my grandfather would stand out in my mind, however full my treasure chest. He was the perfect grandfather, with white hair and a bushy moustache. Best of all, he had a wooden leg. We sat on the back seat of the coach that was taking us home to London and grandfather sang songs, beating time with that leg of his. The other passengers joined in, and everyone laughed and joked. It was a wonderful experience for me, and I was sure for a long time afterwards that grandfathers were God's gift to children.

* * * * * *

It's worth saying one or two things about the final return home. We seemed to become Londoners again in a few weeks, adjusting our accents and our ways without effort. On all sides we heard pleasant stories of evacuation, of lasting friendships that had been formed, of good times that had been had. I cannot remember hearing a single unhappy story, though surrounded by children who had been evacuees. It seems a remarkable tribute to the people who looked after us.

LESLIE DUNKLING

The Penny Fiddle

Yesterday I bought a penny fiddle
And put it to my chin to play;
But I found the strings were painted
So I threw my fiddle away.

A little red man found my fiddle
As it lay abandoned there,
He asked me if he might keep it,
And I told him I did not care.

But he drew such music from the fiddle
With the help of a farthing bow
That I offered him five guineas for the secret
But alas, he would never let it go.

ROBERT GRAVES

Singing in the Rain

As crowds of people surge along the pavements of our busy cities, we can still find the occasional off-beat figure, sometimes singing a song, sometimes playing an instrument, sometimes dancing to an easy rhythm. Street musicians, or buskers, provide a pleasing contrast to the relentless routine of a working day. As well as

entertaining, they are a visible reminder of a great tradition that goes back far into history.

From the history of Rome in the third century BC there are accounts of a variety of street entertainers. These ranged from composers of verse about current events to groups of travelling players who acted out dramas, in mime, in the street. The authorities approved of these diversions because they kept the crowds happy. The people of Rome were delighted to throw a few coins to these players. From time to time some maimed soldier or sailor sang for a living and the crowds paid him also, perhaps to stop his sad song that drew attention to his misfortune.

In the Middle Ages, the wandering minstrels were a feature of life throughout Europe, and their songs kept alive the deeds of heroes and great battles. Sometimes minstrels were fortunate enough to gain constant employment at the court of a king or a wealthy nobleman. There they sang ballads to entertain their lord as well as to commemorate the history of his family.

King Edward I of England employed twenty-seven such minstrels, or troubadours, and at a great feast he gave in 1306 in honour of his son, the Prince of Wales, there were a hundred minstrels present to celebrate the occasion.

Less fortunate entertainers had to roam the country-side making up ballads, both heroic and comic, to attract the crowds of people flocking to the local fairs and markets. Others provided juggling acts or acrobatic acts, and some set themselves up as herbalists or 'quack'

doctors, selling remedies for all kinds of ills. Sometimes they offered to pull teeth for those who were either brave or in great pain.

The travelling players in sixteenth and seventeenth century England were the forerunners of modern touring theatrical companies. They played in the courtyards of the country inns and on village greens and did much to keep drama alive.

Despite various attempts to ban street entertainers, they have survived to the present day. They turn up in the long, twisting corridors of the London Underground, at open markets, or outside cinemas where they provide humble entertainment for queues waiting to see some mighty epic film. Musicians in pubs are perhaps the present day equivalent of the resident minstrel in the castles of long ago.

In a world that seems to want to make us all the same, to iron out all interesting differences, the busker, singing in the rain, is part of a lively tradition to be cherished.

Adapted from *The Buskers*
by D. Cohen and B. Greenwood

The Fiddler

I got up and dressed, stuck my violin under my jacket, and went out into the streets to try my luck. It was now or never. I must face it now, or pack up and go back home. I wandered about for an hour looking for a likely spot, feeling as though I were about to commit a crime. Then I stopped at last under a bridge near the station and decided to have a go.

I felt tense and shaky. It was the first time, after all. I drew the violin from my coat like a gun. It was here, in Southampton, with trains rattling overhead, that I was about to declare myself. One moment I was part of the hurrying crowds, the next I stood nakedly apart, my back to the wall, my hat on the pavement before me, the violin under my chin.

The first notes I played were loud and raw, like a hoarse declaration of protest, then they settled down and began to run more smoothly and to stay more or less in tune. To my surprise, I was neither arrested nor told to shut up. Indeed, nobody took any notice at all. Then an old man, without stopping, surreptitiously tossed a penny into my hat as though getting rid of some guilty evidence.

Other pennies followed, slowly but steadily, dropped by shadows who appeared not to see or hear me. It was as though the note of the fiddle touched some subconscious nerve that had to be answered – like a baby's cry. When I'd finished the first tune there was over a shilling in my hat: it seemed too easy, like a confidence trick. But I was

SALE OF WORK

elated now; I felt that wherever I went from here this was a trick I could always live by.

I worked the streets of Southampton for several days, gradually acquiring the truths of the trade. Obvious enough to old-timers, and simple, once learnt, I had to get them by trial and error. It was not a good thing, for instance, to let the hat fill up with money – the sight could discourage the patron; nor was it wise to empty it completely, which could also confuse him, giving him no hint as to where to drop his money. Placing a couple of pennies in the hat to start the thing going soon became an unvarying ritual; making sure, between tunes, to take off the cream, but always leaving two pennies behind.

Slow melodies were best, encouraging people to dawdle (Irish jigs sent them whizzing past); but it also seemed wise to play as well as one was able rather than to ape the dirge of the professional waif. To arouse pity or guilt was always good for a penny, but that was as far as it got you; while a tuneful appeal to the ear, played with sober zest, might often be rewarded with silver.

Old ladies were most generous, and so were women with children, shopgirls, typists and barmaids. As for the men: heavy drinkers were always receptive, so were big chaps with muscles, bookies, and punters. But never a man with a bowler, briefcase, or dog; respectable types were the tightest of all. Except for retired army officers, who would bark, "Why aren't you working, young man?" then over-tip to hide their confusion.

Certain tunes, I discovered, always raised a response, while others touched off nothing at all. The most fruitful

were invariably the tea-room classics and certain of the juicier national ballads. 'Loch Lomond', 'Wales! Wales!' and 'The Rose of Tralee' called up their supporters from any crowd – as did 'Largo', 'Ave Maria', Toselli's 'Serenade' and 'The Whistler and His Dog'. The least rewarding, as I said, was anything quick or flashy, such as 'The Devil's Trill' or 'Picking up Sticks', which seemed to throw the pedestrian right out of his stride and completely shatter his charitable rhythm.

All in all, my apprenticeship proved profitable and easy, and I soon lost my pavement nerves. It became a greedy pleasure to go out into the streets, to take up my stand by the station or market, and start sawing away at some moony melody and watch the pennies and halfpennies grow. Those first days in Southampton were a kind of obsession; I was out in the streets from morning till night, moving from pitch to pitch in a gold-dust fever, playing till the tips of my fingers burned.

When I judged Southampton to have taken as much as it could, I decided to move on eastwards. Already I felt like a veteran, and on my way out of town I went into a booth to have my photograph taken. The picture was developed in a bucket in less than a minute, and has lasted over thirty years. I still have a copy before me of that summer ghost. He wears a sloppy slouch hat, heavy boots, baggy trousers, tent and fiddle slung over his shoulders.

From *As I Walked Out One Midsummer Morning*
by Laurie Lee

The Busker

Karen Hunter believes in the magic of pantomime.

Two years ago, she was busking in the Shawlands shopping arcade, Glasgow, playing her violin, her only valuable possession, and making a wish that someone important would hear her.

In the best panto tradition, someone did – the wife of a producer at Scottish Television. She was so impressed with Karen's playing that she asked her for her name and address. But then, also in the tradition of fairy stories, there was a setback. The piece of paper with the address was lost and Karen went on busking.

The good fairy must have been watching over her, however, as, many months later, Karen, a student at the Royal Scottish Academy of Music and Drama, went along for an audition at STV as part of a group of fellow students. The producer remembered her and booked her as a solo artist.

Since then Karen has had many engagements on television. This brought her to the notice of the producer of *Dick Whittington*, the pantomime that opens at the Pavilion Theatre, Glasgow, next Wednesday. He sent out his magic carpet to collect her and now Karen is a member of the cast.

She will be playing the part of the ship's mate and will be playing some lively tunes in the show.

From the *Glasgow Herald*

The Piper

Street musician claims he's the new Pied Piper

When John Collins, an unemployed
labourer, appeared in court yesterday
he made this startling claim to
equally startled officials. Collins had
been charged with 'causing an ob-
struction and creating a nuisance in a
busy thoroughfare,' a charge he
roundly denied.
"How could I be causing an ob-
struction when people were enjoying
themselves and were willing to give
me money," claimed Collins. "Even
the people in the shops were nipping
out to hear me."
It was pointed out that the noise he
was creating by playing the bagpipes
in the middle of a busy precinct could
be considered a nuisance. Collins
replied, "I never thought I'd see the
day when a Scottish judge, in a Scottish court, would suggest that playing
bagpipes was a nuisance."
Collins was admonished and afterwards spoke to our reporter who
suggested that he did not sound
Scottish.
"I'm an adopted Scot," said Collins in a heavy Midlands accent.
"The people here are very generous
and I come up at this time every year
to entertain the holiday crowds. The
children love to listen to me. I've got
a big following among them, just like
the Pied Piper.
"I play everything on the bagpipes.
'Scotland the Brave', 'Jesus Loves
me', 'Mull of Kintyre'. Anything
they ask for.
"I had some competition the other
day. I came along to my lunch-time
stance and found that two young
ladies were just about to start playing
– a flute, a violin and music. Music!
Can you believe it? Imagine a busker
with music.
"Maybe they were students trying
to earn some extra cash. I don't
know. Anyway, I gave a few blasts on
the pipes of 'Heiland Laddie' and
that sent them packing. But it didn't
do me much good. I had just got
going with a few coins in my cap
when I was moved on by the law.
"It's no joke trying to earn an
honest penny nowadays," said our
modern Pied Piper as he moved off,
whistling a few bars of 'The Skye
Boat Song'.

The Street Musician

With plaintive fluting, sad and slow,
The old man by the roadside stands.
Who would have thought such notes could flow
From such cracked lips and withered hands.

On shivering legs he stoops and sways,
And not a passer stops to hark;
No penny cheers him as he plays;
About his feet the mongrels bark.

But piping through the bitter weather,
He lets the world go on its way.
Old piper! Let us go together,
And I will sing and you shall play.

JAMES REEVES

Snow

The time I like best
is 6 a.m.
and the snow is six inches deep.

Which I'm yet to discover
'cos I'm under the cover
and fast fast asleep.

Our street is dead lazy
especially in winter.
Some mornings you wake up
and it's lying there
saying nothing. Huddled
under its white counterpane.

But soon the lorries arrive
like angry mums,
pull back the blankets
and send it shivering
off to work.

To
boggan
or not
to boggan?
That is the question.

Winter
morning.
Snowflakes
for breakfast.
The street
outside
quiet
as a
long
white
bandage.

From *Sky in the Pie* by ROGER McGOUGH

The Wonder of Snow

It has snowed all night and the evergreens are holding up thick fists of snow like boxing gloves.

On other trees long twigs, thin as wire, serve as the base for high walls of snow. The laying of the pure white bricks on the clear black boughs has been so gentle, and each brick in itself so light that a perfect balance is achieved.

We shall not encounter a more delicate miracle than the birth of snow ....

Now see those falling flakes.
The feeble filigrees, the fairy ferns descend.
They stick and stay where they have fallen.
Now an inch, now a foot, many feet at last.
A hush, a pause, as the soundless feathers fall.
The roads become empty and traffic comes to a halt.
Civilisation has been stilled.
Silence has fallen.
These, the frailest of all earthly envelopes and
perhaps the most beautiful, have yet the power
to bestow peace upon the world.

From *The Wonder of Snow*
by JOHN STEWART COLLIS

Snow Flakes and Snow Falls

Snow flakes form when water vapour condenses at a temperature below freezing point. But the mystery of snow-crystals is that no two are ever alike. When one considers the millions of crystals that fall in a snowstorm, this is an amazing feat of nature.

Every one of these beautiful snow-crystals is six-sided and the simple shapes that form seem to grow by magic into more elaborate designs. When the weather is very cold the snow will fall in separate dry powdery flakes which can be taken and carefully examined. You must not confuse a snow flake with a snow-crystal, as a flake is made up of a large number of crystals. One flake, in fact, may sometimes comprise two or three dozen crystals.

Snow flakes are fluffy and irregular. As they pile up, air pockets form between the starry points and arms. If you could melt 10cm of snow, you would have only 1cm of water. The rest is air. This trapped air makes the snow very light.

Some snow flakes have sharper points than others. This makes them cling to each other. On a twig no thicker than a pencil, these snow flakes may pile up 5 or 8cm high. On top of a fencepost you may see 12 or 15cm of snow flakes. Even electric wires can hold an 8cm layer.

Snow falls have two opposite results, they can create confusion and difficulty, or give much benefit. We all know the chaos that they can cause to road and rail transport, but on the other hand snow provides a very valuable blanket over the land and protects growing seeds and vegetation from extreme cold. Without the snow blanket many plants would be killed. Snow is a poor conductor of heat and therefore keeps the warmth in and the cold out; this also explains why we often hear of sheep being rescued alive from deep snow-drifts after being buried for several days.

There has been recorded a difference of as much as 50 degrees between the top and the bottom of a snow blanket.

As more and more snow falls, the lower layers of snow are compressed and gradually, as the air is forced out, they turn to solid ice.

Lost

Whenever I see light feathers of snow moving slowly down a window to make a white pillow on the sill, and hear the thin moan of wind through casement cracks in a room where a fireplace is singing with flames, I remember the Christmas when I was nine, and our house at Indian Willows.

We were lost. I knew that from the cold sound of my father's voice. He was angry, he shouted at me and then at my little brother, Louis. If he had known where he was he would have been confident and joked with us.

We were in the family car, driving deep into the country. When the first snow started to fall and the car swerved on the icy road, Father hunched over the wheel and growled. The land was white and the sky dark. I was worried – because he was. I did not know what I could do to cheer him up. And the cold in the car's back seat made my fear worse.

We left the city on a cold morning. It was so early the street lights were still on, solitary yellow beacons in the empty avenues. We drove through the darkness like people escaping. We had brought a picnic lunch, which we ate in the parked car at the roadside, and all through lunch Father had studied a map while Mother fed us sandwiches.

Later in the afternoon, on a narrow road, the snow began – first a flurry, then clouds of small sweeping flakes. With the snow it grew dark. The houses and stores we passed were shut, their windows unlighted, like blind eyes.

I said, “Can we stop and buy something?” I did not want to buy anything. I wanted to know why those buildings were deserted.

“Impossible. They’re only open in the summer,” said Father.

Summer seemed so distant. The long drive and the winter cold were making me feel sick. I envied Louis, who was fast asleep and snoring, with his hands in his pockets.

“Why –?” I started to say. It was then that Father shouted at us to be quiet. Mother reached back and stroked my hair. I knew that Father was lost. This made him seem angry, but really he was worried.

“There’s a hotel,” said Mother.

“Closed for the winter,” said Father, and he swore. He did it forcefully, spitting out the words he told us we should never say.

The car slowed down. Ahead, through the snow tumbling in the headlights, I saw a fork in the road.

Mother rattled the map. She said, “I can’t figure this out.”

“Go left,” I said.

Father turned around and said, “Why?”

The road on the left was wider. It had tyre marks and telephone poles and a very secure fence. It looked safe. But I did not know how to explain this. On wide roads I felt as if we were heading home, on narrower ones I doubted that we would ever arrive, and there were some small roads on which I felt we would disappear – just ahead – where the road seemed to end.

I said, “Because there are signs on that one.”

"We've been driving for hours," said Mother.

"I think Marcel has a point – about those signs," said Father. He took the left fork.

The snow was deep on this new road, and it was still falling. We were travelling down a tunnel that was white and collapsing softly upon us. The car slipped sideways and Father cursed. I was too afraid to move and warm myself. I prayed that we would arrive soon.

I had always trusted Father. He was funny, he was strong, he had made long and difficult journeys. But today he seemed different, somewhat confused by the snowstorm and uncertain of the road.

A storm to me then was simply terror and unusual noises. It was the pain in my toes from the aching cold, the stale smell of the car; it was delay. I was car-sick, I was impatient, I was sorry we had come. I had not really known why I had not wanted to leave home. Now I knew. The snow was relentless – it blocked the windows and made the wipers spank the frames. It was the reason we were alone on the road. We should not be here, I thought. This snow, these woods, this wobbling ride – it might never end.

And there was something else that I was almost too fearful to think: that my father – as reckless as he was brave – was doing something foolishly wrong, that he was misbehaving or breaking some law. He knew better than to lead us through this storm. But he had sneaked us away from home and now he was lost and so we were all lost.

Mother said, "It's so dark – do you think we have far to go?"

"Ask Marcel," said Father sharply. "He's the one who told me to take a left."

"Don't be childish," said Mother. She often said this to him when he upset her.

"It's not far," I said. I saw birds huddled in the trees at the roadside, roosting in the branches. This frightened me – even the birds knew better than to travel in a snowstorm. And under each dark tree was a darker thing, like a panther, a sleek humpbacked shadow with its wicked face lowered in the snow, watching us pass.

"Look," said Louis, waking and yawning, "a light. Is that our house?"

"No," said Father. "But let's stop and get directions."

The light flickered like fire.

"What is the light doing?" asked Louis.

Father was silent. He eased the car off the road into the driveway of a house so tall it rose like a chimney, upward into the stormy night. The snow appeared to fall from its upper storeys. It had a porch and an empty trellis, but its narrow windows glowed brightly and the light, as much a warning as a welcome, made it stranger than if it had been in total darkness.

Mother said, "Is it a hotel?"

"It looks that way," said Father. "I can't imagine why it's still open. Maybe there's someone inside who knows where we are."

He turned off the engine and walked towards the house through the troughs of snow. And he vanished inside.

From *A Christmas Card*
by Paul Theroux

. . . and Found

The snowfall became a blizzard with winds gusting to 200 kilometres per hour. Snow pounding out of the skies packed into perilously unstable masses. Avalanche danger soared. On March 30, 1982, Alpine Meadows closed its mountain; the next day it ordered most of its employees home.

In spite of the extreme hazard that afternoon, Anna Conrad and visiting friend Frank Yeatmen decided to ski the half mile from her house to the ski area. As they approached, mountain manager Bernie Kingery watched grimly, then called Anna into the ski-patrol office and lectured her on the incredibly dangerous thing she had just done. When Bernie finished, Anna went back to the locker room, looking for Frank.

It was at that moment – on the afternoon of March 31 – that the avalanche thundered down the mountain. Shock waves hit first. Massive steel beams flexed, bending and twisting as if made of rubber. As snow-laden wind shrieked through, the structure exploded. A third force, rampaging snow, destroyed almost everything still standing.

When the avalanche struck, a row of heavy wooden lockers crashed down on Anna, injuring her head. Instead of crushing her, however, they fell across a wooden bench, forming a five-foot-long, two-foot-high space in the snow. Anna woke to find herself wrapped in a cocoon of snow and wood. "It was black; I had no idea where I was or what had happened." She also had no way of

gauging the passage of time. For perhaps twenty-four hours she drifted between unconsciousness and agonising periods of wakefulness.

Some time on April 1, she found some matches. Lighting them, she discovered names on the lockers above her. Finally she knew where she was. But, more important, she had discovered a defence against the cold. "I kept pulling clothes out of lockers whenever I felt chilly." When Anna was rescued, she had on three pairs of ski pants. Her diet, though, had been meagre – snow.

The effort to rescue Anna and the others had begun on March 31, when dogs were brought in to help 150 searchers. Bridget, a German shepherd, caught Anna's scent and led a search party to her tomb on Friday, April 2.

"I heard voices yelling, 'Anna, Anna, are you down there?' And I yelled back, 'I sure am.' But they never heard me," she recalled. Then the voices stopped, and Anna could hear the muffled crunch of snow as the searchers walked away.

Unknown to Anna, the snowstorm had turned vicious again, increasing avalanche danger and aborting all rescue efforts. Two days passed. Finally, on Monday, April 5, Anna heard once again the sounds of human activity above her. She knew she couldn't survive much longer; running out of snow to eat, she could feel herself becoming increasingly dehydrated. "I was just grabbing snow and eating it as fast as I could .... I also prayed a lot that day."

Once again, Bridget had caught her scent, the first time

in North America that an avalanche dog had found a person alive. Fifteen searchers, working three metres above her, began removing debris. "All of a sudden," Anna remembered, "there was a small area where some light shone through, and I saw snow sifting in. I was thirsty, and snow meant water! I grabbed for it." When her rescuers saw her hand, one shouted: "Anna, is that you?"

"I'm OK, I'm alive," Anna called back.

As the debris was being stripped away, Bernard Courdurier reached into the hole to hold Anna's hand. Then she was given oxygen. Gently the young woman was lifted into a waiting helicopter. As the aircraft lifted off the ground, a tumultuous cheer came from the searchers, so loud Anna heard it above the roar of the jet helicopter.

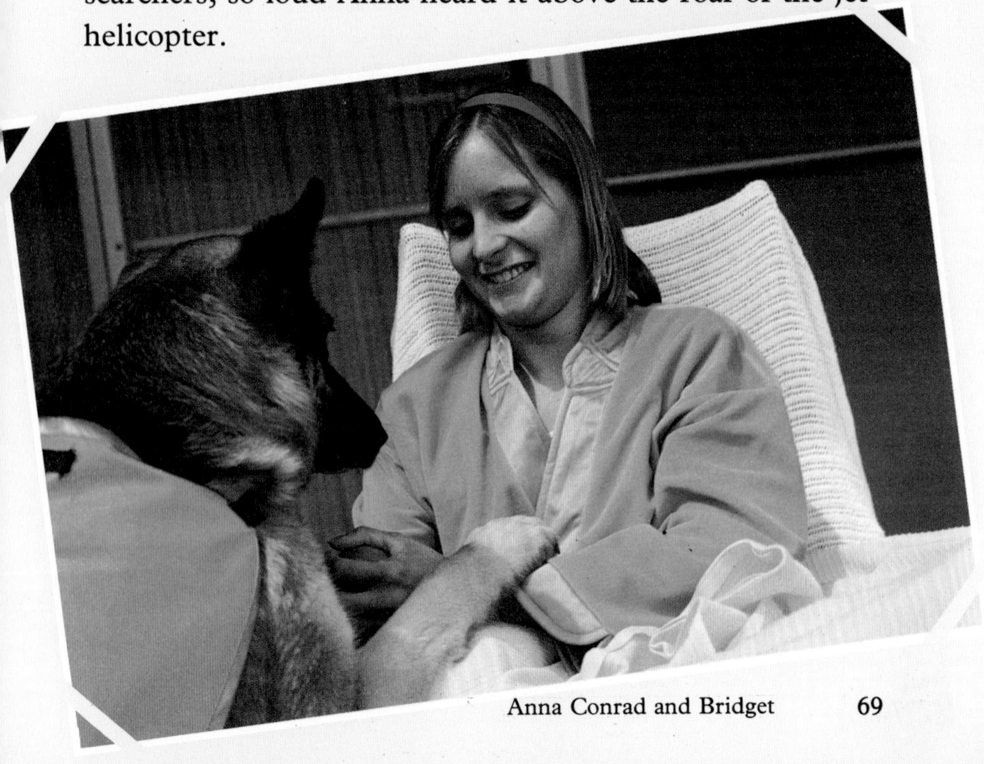

Anna Conrad and Bridget

Looking down, she saw, for the first time, the havoc of the storm. A stark steel skeleton was all that remained of the summit terminal building. Wreckage covered five acres. Huge trees had snapped off like toothpicks; snow was piled six metres high. The magnitude of damage was beyond anything even imagined.

The nightmarish experience cost Anna much of her left foot and all of her right foot. But unlike seven others, Anna survived.

From an article by DAVID CUPP in the *National Geographic Magazine*

Cat and the Weather

Cat takes a look at the weather.
Snow.
Puts a paw on the sill.
His perch is piled, is a pillow.

Shape of his pad appears.
Will it dig? No.
Not like sand.
Like his fur almost.

But licked, not liked.
Too cold.
Insects are flying, fainting down.
He'll try

to bat one against the pane.
They have no body and no buzz.
And now his feet are wet:
it's a puzzle.

Shakes each leg,
then shakes his skin
to get the white flies off.
Looks for his tail,

tells it to come on in
by the radiator.
World's turned queer
somehow. All white,

no smell. Well, here
inside it's still familiar.
He'll go to sleep until
it puts itself right.

MAY SWENSON

Snow~Siege

"I can smell snow," Jessie would say with a shiver when the weather became icy cold. "We're in for't!"

It was fun at first when the snow began to fall, great flat flakes floating from the sky like soft feathers. They settled gently on the hedges and trees, quietly piling one on top of the other till the whole farm was transformed into a dazzling white wilderness.

Sometimes the storm came on silently in the dead of night, taking us by surprise. When we woke in the morning we knew by the ominous hush that something had happened. Every sound was muffled as though the world had fallen asleep; and when we looked out of the window we could see nothing but great wreaths of snow. Everything looked fresh and new.

At other times it started with a blizzard. The wind wailed and howled as it blew the icy flakes horizontally against the window-panes. They froze where they landed, blotting out the light; and we knew that the storm was here to stay.

At first, while it was still possible to get out of doors, I was in my element. No going to school; every day a holiday with the snow for my plaything. Plenty of sledging and snowballing; the thrill of seeing everything take on a sudden soft beauty. Everywhere one looked there was a lovely sight to see. Even the cart-shed became a fairy-tale castle and the tattie-bogles looked like snowmen.

There was the excitement, too, of feeling marooned. It was an adventure, like living in a story book.

But gradually, as the farm-road became blocked and the snow relentlessly hemmed us in, I began to hate the sight of the great white wreaths that loomed over us, growing higher and wider every day. They took on monstrous

shapes, like grotesque Polar beasts threatening to creep closer and swallow us up. What if we were lost for ever under a suffocating snow blanket?

For weeks on end there was no sign of the postie, the van-man, or any human being from the outside world. No hope of even venturing outside the door. Often the hinds had to dig away the drifts before we could push it open. They made long tunnels to the steading and the byre, but it was a never-ending task, for the snow soon filled them up again. Even when it had stopped falling it had frozen so hard that we were sealed in, and there was nothing for us to do but bide our time and wait for the thaw.

The worst moment came when the telephone-wires broke under the weight of snow and our last link with the outside world was gone.

From *A Breath of Border Air*
by Lavinia Derwent

Drip, Drip, Drip

Every day we waited impatiently for the thaw but it seemed reluctant to come.

When it did, it was even more uncomfortable than the storm. Nothing on earth can be more miserable than a 'cold thaw', with everything looking bleak and the snow drip-drip-dripping as it slowly melts away. Jessie had to hound me out of the house.

"Awa' ootbye an' get some colour into your cheeks. Ye're a peely-wally object!"

Though I had been gasping for fresh air, the discomfort of slopping about in the slush was so great that I clung, shivering, to the fireside.

The snow began to look old and dirty. Soon it ran like rivers, oozing under the kitchen door, into the hall, and all over the place. Water seemed to cascade everywhere, from burst pipes, from melting icicles, from rooftops when the snow came thudding down like an avalanche. I had to be careful not to get buried under it for it could have felled me to the ground.

There were times when I longed for it to freeze again so that everything could be neat and clean. But gradually I could see patches of black earth and sense the first faint signs of spring. The cocks and hens emerged from the hen-houses to begin their clucking and pecking, and soon the whole farm stirred to life once more.

From *A Breath of Border Air*
by LAVINIA DERWENT

Wet

Wet wet wet
the world of melting winter,
icicles weeping themselves away
on the eaves
little brown rivers streaming
down the road
nibbling
at the edges of the tired snow,
    all puddled mud
    not a dry place to put
    a booted foot,
everything
    dripping
    slipping
    gushing
    slushing
and listen to that brook
rushing
like a puppy loosed from its leash.

LILIAN MOORE

Strad

Julian Lloyd Webber is the owner of one of the most expensive musical instruments in the world, a 300 year old Stradivarius cello that cost £192 500. Strad, as Julian calls his cello, causes him certain problems, like paying £700 per year for insurance. But travel by air is Strad's real problem, as Julian explained.

"Airlines demand a full passenger fare if a cellist wants to bring his instrument into the cabin. If it goes into the hold they will not accept responsibility for it.

"A few years back I went to Dublin and asked if I could keep the old cello with me. I was told to pay full fare, and I pleaded that it should go half fare as it did not eat, drink or smoke and was quieter than other passengers.

"I refuse to pay full fare because you can always put a cello somewhere in a plane, even in with the crew's coats.

"I was told if I was allowed to bring my cello on, every passenger would want to. I told them it was unlikely that 200 passengers owned cellos. But eventually I gave in and it travelled in the hold.

"I opened my case at the other end, and the cello's ebony fingerboard had completely broken off."

At Amsterdam a hostess told him that he could not bring 'THAT' on, or the next passenger would want to carry a piano.

"A grand piano," Julian said, "does not fit in a seat like a cello." The hostess, however, was adamant. "You can get pianos these days," she added triumphantly, "which fold up."

The great cellist, Rostropovitch, unlike Julian Lloyd Webber, was prepared to pay for a full ticket for his cello. But he found it always had to make way for a passenger if the plane was over-booked.

"Cunningly," explained Julian, "he then booked his cello as Miss or Ms Cello and that guaranteed the seat."

Julian has now discovered ways of getting his instrument into the cabin, but he said, "They are secret ways, and if I told you, my game would be up."

Whatever happens when he boards a plane, Julian can guarantee he will always be searched before he gets off.

"Seeing a giant cello case makes the Customs men suspicious. The funny thing is, they often search the cello but not my baggage.

"In Sweden the guy thought he was really on to something, and when he could not find anything, he insisted I proved to him I was a cellist.

"So I got it out, let down the spike (leg), and sat down and played Bach. I rarely play Bach in public, so he got an exclusive preview."

From the *Daily Express*

Problem Solved

Bass that comes to bits for travelling

Dutch jazzman Arnold Dooyweert says of his customised double bass: "This isn't something you can buy in a shop."

Mr Dooyweert, who has been appearing in Scotland this week with the Tom Varner Quartet, made the alterations to the bass himself.

"Two bolts hold the neck on to the body, and the sound-post is now fixed on with nails," he said. "If the instrument-maker could see it now, he would faint."

His reason? "Every time I went on a plane I had to buy a seat for it. After one trip to Munich, when it came off the plane in pieces, I decided to take matters into my own hands."

From *The Glasgow Herald*

Mr Timothy Pringle

Mr Timothy Pringle
Lived on his own
As he was single.
Returning from work
In the evening gloom
He found an elephant
In his room.
It had a label
Round its neck
"My name is Doris
Eileen Beck".
Even if the name was Jim
It didn't really help poor Tim.
Is that elephant a her or he?
Asked Mrs Screws (the landlady).
Tim said "It's a female elephant, why?"
"No women in rooms," was the stern reply.

SPIKE MILLIGAN

Percy the Pest

Percy was a liar,
Percy was a pest.
So they bought a one way ticket
and packed him off to Jest –
Where many a true word is spoken.

GRIMSDYKE CHURCHFOREST

" You heard correctly, Madam. I DID say I would rather fly to the States inside that whale, than in the same plane as you and your revolting children."

Flying Whale

he whale in question was Ramu, en ›ute to California from Windsor afari Park, where, until yesterday, he ›as the 'star turn'.

And thereby hangs a sad tale. For ›hen you get through, as Ramu does, 0 kilograms of mackerel between reakfast and suppertime, something's got to give.

What gave was the space in his play ool. At $4\frac{1}{2}$ tonnes and 6 metres, the tar could hardly turn round any onger.

He had to go.

His destination: A million-gallon ool in San Diego, big enough for ven the biggest of mammals.

"We're sorry," said Ronnie Smart, nanaging director of the Safari Park, 'but it would have been unfair to keep im any longer."

Operation Flying Whale began as lawn broke over Berkshire.

First the roof had to be stripped rom Ramu's pool. Then a huge crane vith a canvas sling hanging from the ib was used to haul him out.

Next came the hard part: getting nine-year-old Ramu to swim into the sling. That took lots of persuasion and eight strong men in wetsuits.

At last he was hauled 9 metres into the air and lowered into an outsize crate lined with foam rubber. Ramu snorted his disapproval.

The VIP treatment followed.

Europe's only captive killer whale was smeared in grease and cod liver oil to keep his skin moist.

He was massaged with packs of ice and sprayed with a hose for good measure.

Safari Park vet David Taylor explained: "Provided we keep his skin nice and damp, a whale can live out of water for several days."

Then came the eye-catching journey from Windsor to Heathrow to catch flight 4054 – inappropriately by Flying Tigers Line.

Getting Ramu aboard the DC-8 wasn't easy. It took a multitude of helpers in varying uniforms, heaving and pushing.

Cries of "Left a bit" and "Mind his tail" filled the air. But one final collective shove and he was aboard for the record-breaking flight.

So you think you've got problems

When Treehorn went into class, his teacher said, "Nursery school is down at the end of the hall, honey."

"I'm Treehorn," said Treehorn.

"If you're Treehorn, why are you so small?" asked the teacher.

"Because I'm shrinking," said Treehorn. "I'm getting smaller."

"Well, I'll let it go for today," said his teacher. "But see that it's taken care of before tomorrow. We don't shrink in this class."

After recess, Treehorn was thirsty, so he went down the hall to the water bubbler. He couldn't reach it, and he tried to jump up high enough. He still couldn't get a drink, but he kept jumping up and down, trying.

His teacher walked by. "Why, Treehorn," she said. "That isn't like you, jumping up and down in the hall. Just because you're shrinking, it does not mean you have special privileges. What if all the children in the *school* started jumping up and down in the halls? I'm afraid you'll have to go to the Principal's office, Treehorn."

So Treehorn went to the Principal's office.

"I'm supposed to see the Principal," said Treehorn to the lady in the Principal's outer office.

"It's a very busy day," said the lady. "Please check here on this form the reason you have to see him. That will save time. Be sure to put your name down, too. That will save time. And write clearly. That will save time."

Treehorn looked at the form:

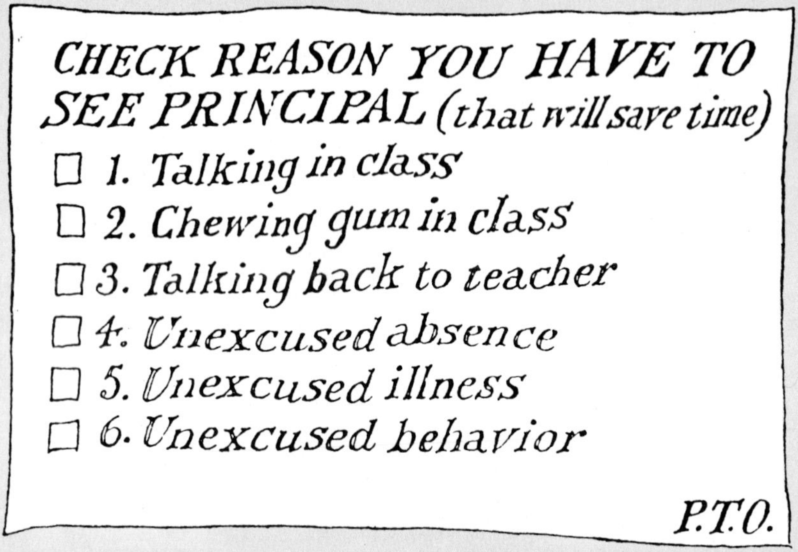

CHECK REASON YOU HAVE TO SEE PRINCIPAL (that will save time)

☐ 1. Talking in class
☐ 2. Chewing gum in class
☐ 3. Talking back to teacher
☐ 4. Unexcused absence
☐ 5. Unexcused illness
☐ 6. Unexcused behavior

P.T.O.

There were many things to check, but Treehorn couldn't find one that said 'Being Too Small to Reach the Water Bubbler'. He finally wrote in 'SHRINKING'.

When the lady said he could see the Principal, Treehorn went into the Principal's office with his form.

The Principal looked at the form, and then he looked at Treehorn. Then he looked at the form again.

"I can't read this," said the Principal. "It looks like SHIRKING. You're not SHIRKING, are you, Treehorn? We can't have any shirkers here, you know. We're a team, and we all have to do our very best."

"It says SHRINKING," said Treehorn. "I'm shrinking."

"Shrinking, eh?" said the Principal. "Well, now, I'm very sorry to hear that, Treehorn. You were right to come to me. That's what I'm here for. To guide. Not to punish, but to guide. To guide all the members of my team. To solve all their problems."

"But I don't have any problems," said Treehorn. "I'm just shrinking."

"Well, I want you to know I'm right here when you need me, Treehorn," said the Principal, "and I'm glad I was here to help you. A team is only as good as its coach, eh?"

The Principal stood up. "Goodbye, Treehorn. If you have any more problems, come straight to me, and I'll help you again. A problem isn't a problem once it's solved, right?"

From *The Shrinking of Treehorn*
by FLORENCE PARRY HEIDE

Seventeen Oranges

I used to be so fond of oranges that I could suck one after another the whole day long – until that time the policeman gave me a scare at the dock gates when he caught me almost redhanded with seventeen hidden away in my various pockets, and he locked me up, and ever since then I've never looked at an orange – because that gave me my fill of them.

I was driving a little pony-and-cart for the Swift Delivery Company in those days, and lots of pick-ups were at the docks, where I could put on a handy sample load and be back at the depot before the other carters had watered their mares.

Now I was not what you call a proper fiddler, and I did not make a practice of knocking things off just because they didn't belong to me, like some people do, but just the same, it was very rare I came off those docks without a bit of something to have a chew at during the day.

Say they were unloading a banana boat; well, I used to draw my little cart alongside. There were often loose bunches that had dropped off the main stalks. And when the chance came I would either make a quick grab, or some friendly foot would shove them towards me. Then I used to duck them out of sight under my brat. The brat was an apron made from a Tate and Lyle sugar-bag, supposed to be a good protection against rain and rough wear, but mine was used mostly for concealment. And for the rest of that day I'd be munching bananas, even though I hadn't a passion for them like I had for oranges.

But mine was all done on the spur of the moment, more or less, and not worked out to a fine art, as in one instance with Clem Jones, who came out of the gates carrying a box.

"What have you got in there?" asked Pongo, who was the bobby on duty.

"A cat," said Clem, "but don't ask me to open it, or the blighter will get away."

"A cat?" said Pongo. "Don't come it. Let's have it opened."

Clem wouldn't at first, but when Pongo insisted, he got mad, and he flung it open, and out leapt a ship's cat, which darted back along the docks with Clem after it, shouting. Two minutes later he came out with the same box, holding the lid down tight and scowling at the grinning Pongo, and all the way home he scowled, until in the privacy of his own kitchen he opened the box and took out a full-sized Dutch cheese.

I got caught because the string of my brat broke, and Pongo, after looking over my load, noticed my somewhat bulging pockets. He made me draw the pony-and-cart to one side, then he took me in his cabin and went through my pockets. There were seventeen oranges in all, and he placed them carefully on the table.

"An example has to be made," he said, "of somebody or other – and I reckon you're the unlucky one. Now, my lad, what have you to say for yourself?"

I said nothing. I was dead frightened, but I forced myself to keep my mouth shut. I had read too many detective stories to make the mistake of blabbing.

Anything you say may be used in evidence against you. I kept that firm in my mind, and I refused to be interrogated. Pongo, who did not care for my attitude, said, "Righto, I'll go and bring a colleague as a witness." And with that he went, carefully locking the door behind him.

I felt awful then. It was the suspense. I looked at the walls, I looked at the door, and I looked at the seventeen oranges, and I looked at my brat with the broken string. I thought of how I would get sacked and get sentenced, and of what my mother would say and my father do.

There was no escape. I was there – and the evidence was there before me on the table – and Pongo had gone for his mate to be a witness. I was ruined for life.

"Oh, my God," I moaned in anguish, "whatever shall I do?"

"*Eat 'em!*" spoke a voice in my head.

"Eh?" I asked. "Eat 'em?"

"*Yeh, that's right,*" replied this inner voice – "*and then the evidence will be gone. But be quick about it.*"

I thought for half a second – then I snatched an orange, peeled it in a jiff, popped it in my mouth, crushed the juice out and swallowed it, swallowing the orange, and I was just about to squirt out the pips when the voice cried:

"*No!*"

"Eh?"

"*You have to swallow them too!*"

"What – the pips?"

"*Yes – peel an' all! Evidence.*"

"Oh – oh, of course", and I forced the pips to the back

of my mouth and took a handful of peel to help get them down my gullet.

"Don't bother to chew," said the voice, *"it's a race against time."*

It certainly was. After that first orange I took out my penknife and slashed the fruit into chunks and gulped them down as fast as I could pick them up.

I was all but full to the brim, with three oranges to go, when I heard Pongo and his mate coming back. With a sigh I gave up, but the voice warned me to guzzle on, suggesting that the more I ate the less evidence there would be – and as luck would have it, Pongo and his mate were detained over checking-up on some outgoing wagons, and since the sigh seemed to have cleared up a sort of traffic-jam in my oesophagus, I set about finishing off those last few, and by the time the key turned in the lock I was consuming the final piece of the seventeen oranges.

"This is him," began Pongo to his mate. "I caught him with his pockets ramjam full of oranges – " He looked at the table. "Hi, where are they?"

"Whew," sniffed his mate, "I can smell 'em."

I never spoke.

Pongo began to search. He looked high and low, went through my pockets, felt at my brat, but of course he found no trace of an orange. Finally he figured out what must have happened, but even then he couldn't believe it.

"*Seventeen* oranges," he kept murmuring – "big 'uns at that! – how has he managed it?" But I said nothing. And he couldn't give me in charge, because he had no

evidence upon which to commit me – and because I suppose he did not want to be laughed at. So all he could do was to vituperate, while I kept my lips shut tight, and then he had to let me go.

When I told Clem Jones about it he said that I had been very slow; he said that I could have sued Pongo for hundreds of pounds because of wrongful detention, if only I had been quick-witted enough. But I never was a vindictive sort, and anyway, it was days and days before I could stand really still and think things out, because those seventeen oranges – peel, pips, and all – kept working away in my inside something shocking.

From *The Goalkeeper's Revenge and Other Stories*
by Bill Naughton

The Uncertain Road

You are not to blame if a man becomes a refugee
You are, if he continues to be one

Exile

"Throughout the history of mankind,
people have been uprooted against their will.
Time and again, lives and values,
built from generation to generation,
have been shattered without warning.
Time and again, people in fear,
individuals or whole groups,
persecuted on account of their
profound convictions,
have had to make a most dramatic decision:
to take the uncertain, even perilous, road
to exile, from home, community and homeland,
from friends and often family,
rather than bear the intolerable burdens
of injustice and oppression . . ."

A refugee would like to have your problems

POUL HARTLING
United Nations High Commissioner for Refugees
Nobel Peace Prize Ceremony, Oslo, 1981

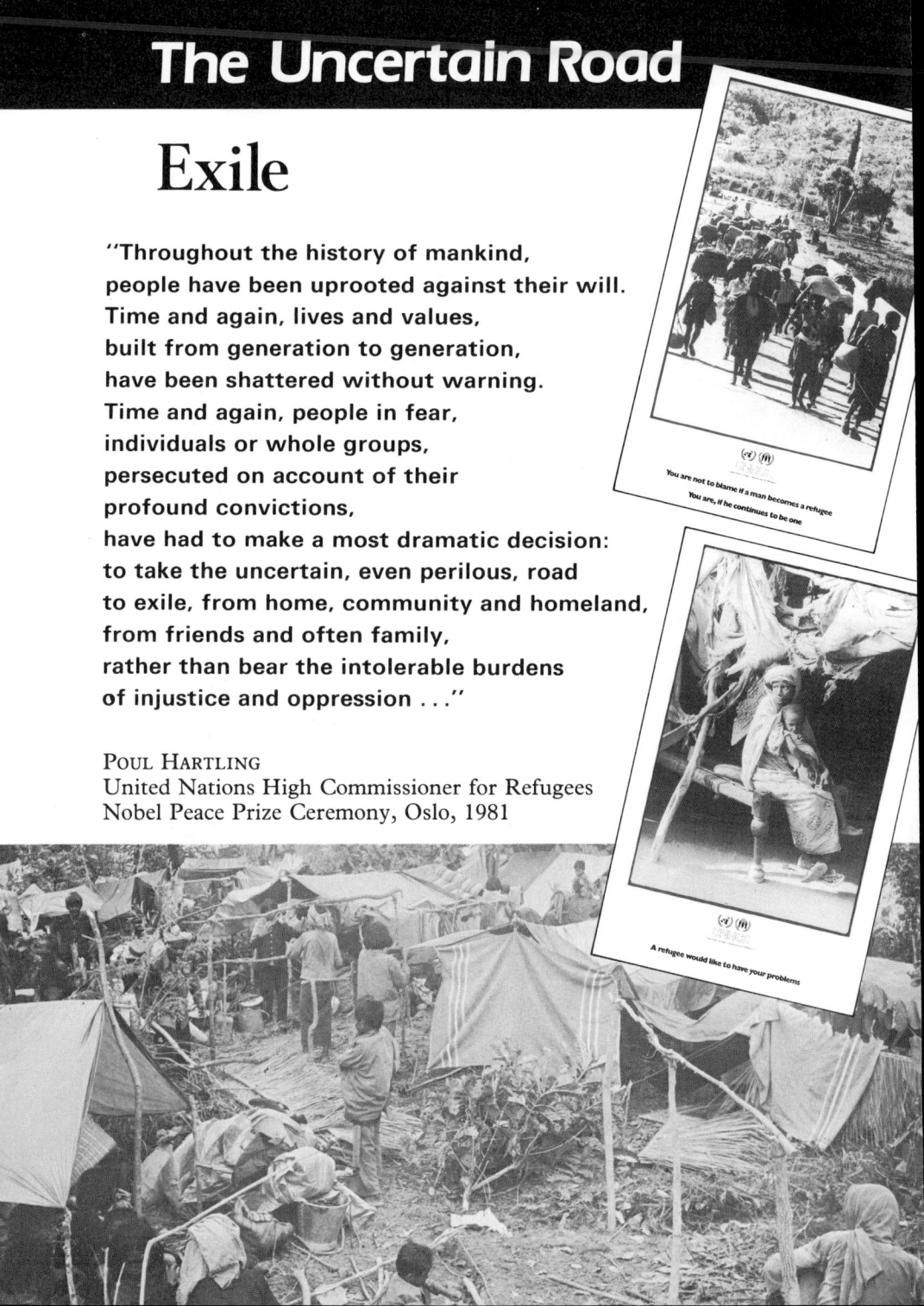

Flight to Freedom

Secret Preparations

One day at the end of August, when the evening meal was finished and the housekeeper had gone home, Tinh got up and quietly closed all the windows of the sitting-room. Le Mai and the children were wondering why, when he spoke to them in his calm voice: "Gather round, I have something to tell you." They came to him and his voice became grave as he went on. "Listen, in about two weeks we are all going to escape, to leave our dear home for ever and sail to Malaysia. From there I shall contact our cousin Ly To in Australia where we shall make our new home. All plans for the journey to Malaysia are made. There will be ninety people in the boat and we shall leave at midnight on the twelfth of September, two nights before full moon. The moon festival will have begun by then and the curfew will be relaxed, so we shall be able to move about without danger from the police."

The children's hearts beat faster as their father spoke. His voice, calm and grave, made the danger feel more real. Hue Hue's one terror was that the police might catch them. She did not give a thought for the voyage, except that she longed for it to start. She could not help, though, feeling sad at the idea of leaving, nor could she bring herself to believe that she would never again see her friends, or their house with all its memories.

Trung, like his mother, said little; his thoughts too were far away. Inside him he was thrilled at the promise

of a new life in Australia. As for Quang and To, they were chattering excitedly about sailing across the sea to Malaysia.

When at last September 12 arrived, the children were packed off to school as usual. As the last class of the afternoon broke up, Hue Hue waved to her friends and called out "Goodbye!", hardly able to believe that it was forever.

The children were all home by 4 p.m. Le Mai gave them rice and sweet pork, telling them: "Eat all you can. We shall be going hungry for the next week." When they had eaten she said to them: "Now go quietly to your rooms and change." Each of the children, and their parents too, had set aside some old, worn clothes in which they could pass as fisher-folk. Hue Hue slipped out of her clean school uniform and changed into a grubby striped blouse and flowery pattern pyjamas over which she pulled an old pair of black cotton trousers. She had kept, too, a blue and white checked cloth jacket, to wear during the cool nights at sea. On her feet she wore leather sandals with a strap over the toes. Le Mai's outfit was similar. The boys had taken off their clean white shirts and their carefully creased blue shorts and thrown them on the bed. Giggling, they pulled on the disguise that Tinh had procured for them and himself, the salt-stained shirt, black trousers and sandals of a typical fisherman.

Like a good clock-maker, Tinh had synchronised all the time-pieces in his house at the correct hour, which was now 5.45 p.m. He called Le Mai and the children to him and motioned them to follow him to the family shrine.

There, for some minutes, they worshipped. Then they stood up and Tinh said: "It's just on six o'clock. You each know what to do. I am leaving now to warn our neighbours, then I shall go straight on to the market place. Keep close enough to remain in sight; act naturally, but be careful."

When it was Hue Hue's turn to leave she ran back to her bedroom. Standing in the doorway she glanced round, fixing in her mind the pale blue walls covered with photos of her family and friends and of her favourite actress Chan Chan. "Goodbye all of you and everything," she thought, and had to force back the tears. Then firmly, Hue Hue shut the door behind her, closed it on her life in Vietnam.

At about half-past six Hue Hue reached the market. Dusk was falling; the night was warm and not a breath of wind stirred the palm trees. Stars were beginning to shine in a cloudless sky. The sound of festive music was coming from the market place. The night was one of the most beautiful that Hue Hue could remember. The moon festival was a festival for children, and so there were many of them in the market place, each with a lantern, eating candy and moon-cake which made Hue Hue's mouth water, while her parents greeted their friends, chatted and laughed. The moon festival seemed to have put everybody in a good mood.

Hue Hue, scanning the crowds for the rest of her family, had no difficulty in spotting them in the glare of the gas-lights. She sat down on the ground and began to chat with her brother Trung.

About twenty paces away, she could just make out her father and mother, seated on a bench with her brothers Quang and To.

It was around eight o'clock when Hue Hue noticed two men walking casually down to where two sampans were moored only a few metres away from her. She nudged Trung. "Look," she whispered, "the signal!"

The Departure

A moment later, out of the crowd, Uncle Ba appeared at her side. He bent down and in a quiet voice said: "Come along Hue Hue and Trung and the rest of you; all aboard!" Others followed, some carrying children, some leading them by the hand, walking towards the sampans.

Soon Hue Hue's sampan, crammed with people, put off into the river and headed downstream; its gunwales were almost level with the water which, at the slightest rolling, came seeping over. Hue Hue was sure it was going to sink, but five minutes later the sampan was bumping along the side of the big boat and Hue Hue, Trung and all the others were climbing aboard up a short wooden ladder. Hue Hue sat down on deck, Trung next to her. She looked round at the faces, dimly visible in the moonlight, to make sure that her parents and brothers were there, and discovered that they were not. She called out to Uncle Ba, who reassured her: "Don't worry, Hue Hue, I'll bring them along with the next lot."

But as Uncle Ba's sampan regained the river bank, he saw Tinh and his family and the rest of the passengers being questioned by a policeman.

Terrified that the escape plan had been discovered, Uncle Ba returned to the big boat. They must leave at once, he decided, and he started the engine. Only when they were moving downstream towards the open sea did Uncle Ba discover that the engineer and the captain had been left behind. There was now no one on board the boat who was competent to sail it.

It was the motion of the boat that awoke Hue Hue. She opened her eyes and realised that Trung was next to her. Drowsily she said: "Hello. Have you seen the others?" But before Trung could reply Hue Hue had realised 'the others' were not there. She burst into tears and her brother, weary after a night on watch, felt himself being carried away by his sister's crying. He, too, began to cry and they sat there, wedged one against the other in the crowd, two unhappy children, utterly lost. After a while Trung took hold of himself.

"Cheer up, Hue Hue," he said, "we'll stick together, whatever happens."

The Empty Sea

Uncle Ba, when he was not steering, tried to put some order into life on board, organising the passengers into groups of about ten and telling them to take special care of the aged and the mothers and children.

But poor Uncle Ba had never been to sea and on

meeting it was at a complete loss. He should have altered course some 90 degrees to the west. That would have put the boat on a course to the Malaysian coast. Instead he swung the helm some 30 degrees eastward and kept straight on into the middle of the most dangerous waters in South-East Asia – the South China Sea.

The first day out the boat began to take water, which the bilge pump spewed back into the sea. Next morning, the engine faltered, picked up, faltered again and stopped. An hour went by, then another as the powerless boat drifted. During that time two merchantmen passed not more than a kilometre away and the people on the roof of the wheelhouse waved energetically. Their efforts were in vain; without a sign of recognition the big ships sailed on their way, while the boat-people hurled insults and curses after them. Nothing that had happened so far had so demoralised them. They felt better when they heard the engine splutter once more into life; a thin cheer went up and the boat was again under way, making about 5 km an hour.

At the end of the second day the boat-people, though they didn't realise it, had almost crossed the main shipping lanes and were heading for an empty desert of water.

That night the engine stopped twice more and each time pandemonium broke out below. Torches flashed and

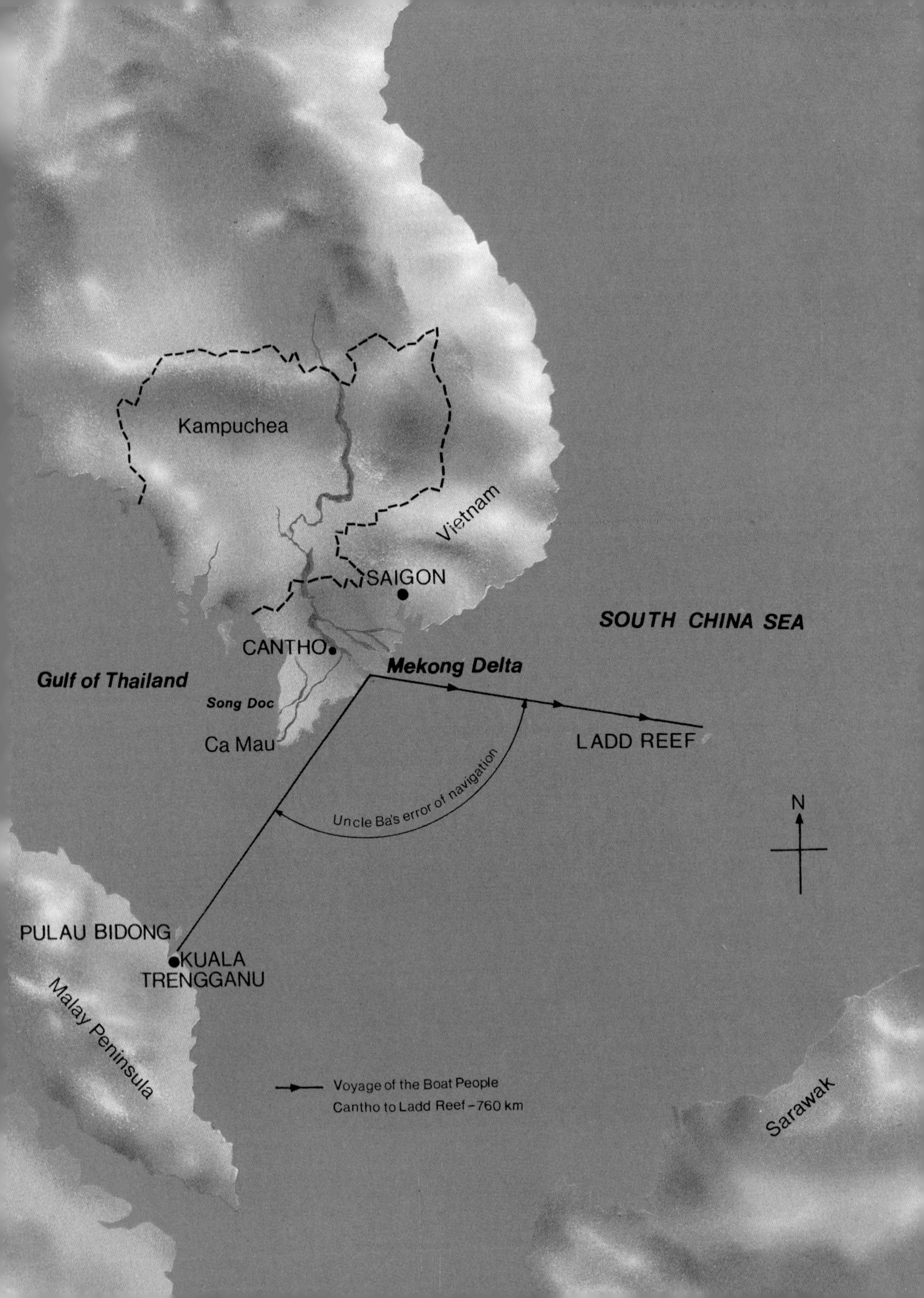

Kampuchea
Vietnam
SAIGON
SOUTH CHINA SEA
CANTHO
Mekong Delta
Gulf of Thailand
Song Doc
Ca Mau
LADD REEF
Uncle Ba's error of navigation
N
PULAU BIDONG
KUALA TRENGGANU
Malay Peninsula
Voyage of the Boat People
Cantho to Ladd Reef – 760 km
Sarawak

buckets were again passed from hand to hand. A gale was blowing up – it was the monsoon season – and the helpless, overloaded boat, tossed here and there by the waves, took so much water that it felt as if it were going to capsize. Then the motor started up, the boat moved forward again and the panic subsided.

All next day the gale blew and torrents of rain, cold and stinging, blotted out the horizon. The engine kept breaking down and each time it did so the boat-people baled for their lives. On deck, the people at the end of the line, lashed by the rain, cold, drenched and exhausted, began to protest. In vain Ba encouraged them: "Come on, stick to it, keep baling or we're lost." Others took their place. For another day and night the boat-people fought the storm and the faulty engine and somehow kept their craft afloat.

Life dragged on painfully through long anxious days and restless nights. Hue Hue's thoughts had dwelt ceaselessly on her parents and brothers back in Vietnam. She was thirteen; she missed them terribly and cried whenever she imagined them at home.

She looked round the crowded deck. Where were they going, all these people, most of them unknown to her? Before them lay nothing but sea, stretching out to the horizon.

The following weeks and months were filled with horror for everyone on the small boat. They ran aground on Ladd Reef, a coral reef one thousand kilometres from their destination. Food ran out. They had to survive on rain water, raw shellfish and seagull meat. One by one the

castaways died of illness or starvation. Many, including her brother, Trung, were drowned. Hue Hue was the sole survivor.

Four months after leaving Vietnam, on the point of starvation and almost too weak to speak, she was found by some fishermen, Gradually she was nursed back to health and eventually was able to go to Australia to begin a new life.

Vietnamese refugees being brought ashore to safety

The Reunion

Meanwhile Tinh and his family, at home in Vietnam, made a second attempt to escape. This time there were no police to turn them back, and finally they reached the island of Pulau Bidong, off the coast of Malaysia.

There, Tinh received a letter dated 5 June 1979 from the Malaysian Red Crescent confirming that Hue Hue was in Australia; "Address unknown. But she knows of your presence in Malaysia and will contact you soon."

Hue Hue, just beginning to come to her senses in her new surroundings, sat down and wrote to her father. She outlined all that had happened since that fateful night in September, nine months before, when they had been separated; told him of Ladd Reef, of Trung's death, and her rescue by the fishermen. She told him too of her new home in Australia and begged him to come quickly with the family to join her.

The letter reached Tinh in mid June. Confronted by this proof of Hue Hue's existence both Le Mai and Tinh cheered up. Their sole aim now was to join her in Australia.

Tinh and his family left Pulau Bidong for the mainland on 13 August. When they reached Kuala Lumpur, Tinh and the boys were installed at the transit camp. Le Mai was taken to hospital. She needed time and peace – impossible to find in a refugee camp – to recover from her sorrow over the loss of her son, Trung. She sadly missed her mother and family in Vietnam too.

In the early afternoon of 25 October, after flying from Kuala Lumpur, they reached their Australian home, a

simply furnished but comfortable ground apartment at the East Hills hostel. They settled in, and leaving the front door open, waited impatiently for Hue Hue who was still at school. Le Mai, tired out after the flight, lay down to rest, her heart racing at the thought of seeing her daughter again.

Hue Hue, with her school books under one arm, stepped off the train at East Hills station. As she walked on in the warm October sun past clumps of blue gum trees her mind was calm. A few minutes more and she would be together again with her family. This was what, for more than a year, she had ceaselessly prayed for; and it was about to happen. God had taken care of everything. She must remember to make her promised offering to the Lord Buddha.

Vietnamese children playing in a refugee camp in Malaysia

At the hostel a little boy stopped her. "They're all waiting for you," he said and led her along the pathway until they were in front of the window of Bellingen 2, where he called out, "Hue Hue's here!" In an instant Quang and To were through the open door. Momentarily they stopped short, so overcome at the sight of their sister that they could only smile at her. Then Tinh was at her side. As she flung her free arm round her father's neck both were crying. Tinh led Hue Hue inside to her mother; she hugged Le Mai, then Quang and To, in a confusion of tears and talk – it did not matter which. Nothing mattered now that they were all together again. All except their beloved Trung. They asked about him and Hue Hue told them quietly, in a few words. For all their joy at her return, their grief for Trung, like hers, remained inconsolable.

Adapted from *The Girl in the White Ship*
by PETER TOWNSEND

Refugees

One of the saddest features of the twentieth century has been the vast number of people who have had to flee from their homeland because of fear of war and persecution. Often these refugees have had to leave everything behind in order to seek safety in another country where they hope to begin a new life.

Refugees can be found in every continent. At the moment there are at least twelve million refugees in the world, and the numbers keep on growing.

The story of Hue Hue tells something about the Boat People of Vietnam. Tens of thousands made the dangerous voyage by sea to seek refuge in Hong Kong, Malaysia and the Philippines. Once they reached those countries they were put in refugee camps before moving on to another country. Similar camps can be found in many other parts of the world.

In these camps a great deal is done to trace families that have been separated in the flight to freedom. Help is also given in contacting relatives in other countries to see if it is possible for the refugees to go there. That is what happened to Soo Min.

This young boy is now at school in the USA after spending nine months in a refugee camp in Hong Kong. Like Hue Hue, he found himself on a boat, separated from his parents. After twelve days at sea he arrived in Hong Kong and was sent to a refugee camp run by the YMCA. There he was given medical attention and learned to speak English. He remembers looking at

pictures of food and learning words like 'hot dog', 'hamburger' and 'pizza'.

Life in the camp was crowded. There were over 2000 people living in an area not much bigger than a football field. They lived in big, tin huts with about 200 people crowded into each hut, sleeping in three-tier bunks. It wasn't ideal, but it was a lot better than the small boat on which he had spent all those dreary days. In the camp they had regular meals and a weekly treat – a visit to the beach where they could play on the sand and go for a swim.

His happiest moment came when he learned that the YMCA people had traced his parents to a camp in Malaysia. Several months later he was able to join them in the USA.

Many of these refugee camps are under the control of the United Nations High Commissioner for Refugees (UNHCR), which has performed a valuable service to refugees for many years. Not only does UNHCR help people who are seeking refuge, it also helps when emergencies occur due to famine, drought, earthquakes and so on. Each year millions of people are affected by these disasters, and UNHCR is able to call upon support from many places. Governments help. So too do organisations like the Red Cross, Save the Children Fund and the YMCA.

He ain't heavy

It's a long, long road from which there is no return,
While we're on the road to there, why not share,
And the load doesn't weigh me down at all.
He ain't heavy. He's my brother.

BOB RUSSELL

What's a Poem, Anyhow?

The grasses and trees
Change their colours;
But to the wave blooms
On broad sea plains
There comes no autumn.

BUNYA YASUHIDE

I fear thee ancient Mariner!
I fear thy skinny hand!
And thou art long, and lank, and brown,
As is the ribbed sea sand.

SAMUEL TAYLOR COLERIDGE

Glory be to God for dappled things –
For skies of couple-colour as a brinded cow.

GERARD MANLEY HOPKINS

Tell me a word
that you've often heard
yet it makes you squint
to see it in print.

D.H. LAWRENCE

A bird in the air, a fish in the sea,
A bonnie wee lassie came singing to me.

TRAD.

anyone lived in a pretty how town,
(with up so floating many bells down)
spring summer autumn winter
he sang his didn't he danced his did.

e e cummings

What's a Poem, Anyhow?

Peter Todd looked at the word again. 'Poem.'

It was a simple enough word. 'Poem.' He repeated it to himself. It had a nice easy ring to it. But why was it so hard to understand?

Peter was puzzled.

His Grade Five English teacher, Mr Howard, had given this homework on Friday. It seemed like an easy enough assignment at first. All you had to do, said Mr Howard, was find the meaning of the word, 'poem'.

Well, Peter didn't worry too much about it. After all he had all weekend to find out. And today was only Saturday. On Saturday Peter usually played hopscotch or pick-up basketball down at the playground.

So he started walking towards the playground. But that 'poem' thing stayed in his head. It was like stuck to his brain like glue. It just wouldn't go away.

While he was walking he saw Sylvia Butters coming up the street. Sylvia was way taller than Peter. She had long, blond pigtails, braces on her teeth and was in Grade Six.

"Hi, Sylvia!" said Peter.

"Hi, squirt," said Sylvia, looking down at Peter and showing her new skipping rope.

"Say, Sylvia," said Peter, "do you know what a poem is?"

"Sure I know what a poem is. *Everybody* knows what a poem is, silly."

"Bet you don't," dared Peter.

"A poem," said Sylvia, "is music with words." And as she said it she giggled and walked away, skipping rope.

"Music with words," repeated Peter in his head. Wow, what would people think of next? And he kept on walking to the playground.

Down at the playground Peter played hopscotch, pick-up basketball and closest-to-the-wall. But he was lousy. Just couldn't concentrate.

All he kept hearing inside his head was that word. Poem. Poem. Poem. Boy, he was really bugged. He wanted so much to ask some of the other kids what the word meant. But he was afraid they'd laugh at him.

Coming home from the playground he stopped at an intersection for a red light. Mr Puchini, the policeman, was there watching the traffic. Peter walked up to him.

"Sir," said Peter, "would you happen to know what a poem is?"

Mr Puchini was a big man with a black moustache and laughing eyes. He looked down at Peter suspiciously for a second. Then he said suddenly,

"Poems is what poets do. So why don't you ask a poet. Me, I'm a cop, see?"

"O.K., I will," yelled Peter, running off to catch the green light. But when he got across the street and was halfway down the next block the thought occurred to him. He couldn't ask a poet what a poem was because he didn't know any poets.

Too bad. He wished he were a poet. Then he wouldn't have such a hard time of it. If he were a poet it would be easy. He would just write something down, any old thing, and that would be a poem!

Peter was so carried away with his idea of being a poet

that he ran all the rest of the way home. When he arrived home he didn't even say hi to his mom but ran right up to his bedroom. He went straight to his desk and rustled up pencil and paper.

He sat there trying to think of a poem. But nothing came. He sharpened his pencil. Then something popped into his head. He wrote it down.

Fudgsickle stick
in the mud

There, he'd done it!

He looked at the words. *fudgsickle stick in the mud.* Well he didn't know if it was a poem *exactly* but it sure looked goofy enough. It made him laugh to think of it.

Bob, Peter's brother, walked in then. Bob was wearing his Little League cap and had his baseball glove on. He was much older than Peter and could whistle very well.

"Hey Bobby," said Peter, "can you tell me something if I show you something?"

"Yeah, kiddo," said Bob like a big guy.

"See this?" Peter said, showing his paper with *fudgsickle stick in the mud* written on it.

"Yeah," said Bob.

"Is that what you'd call a poem?"

Bobby looked at the words and squinted. He held the paper sideways, upside down and at an angle. Then he shouted:

"Fudgsickle stick in the mud. That's not a poem, stupid!" And he walked right out of the room shaking his head.

For the rest of the day Peter didn't ask another soul about 'poem'. He was too angry. And depressed. Yet as soon as he fell off to sleep that night the word came to him in his dreams. Poem. He saw it lit up in colour on a neon sign. Poem. He saw it on a poster in a parade. Poem. He saw it written in chalk on the road with rain coming down on it. When he woke up it was light and the sun of a bright Sunday was beaming through the bedroom window. His mother walked in smiling.

"Rise and shine, sleepyhead," she said, "everybody else is up and waiting for you to come down to breakfast."

Peter slipped out of bed and started to dress. His mother helped him put his shoes on and lace them.

"Mom," he said, "what's a poem?"

"Oh, a poem is something sweet, or sentimental. Or true. A poem is something that's fun to say," she said.

"Like what?" asked Peter.

Peter's mom thought for a second, her eyes looking up at the corner of the ceiling. Then she recited:

> Down by the river,
> Carved on a rock,
> Three little words,
> Forget me not.

Peter repeated the verse. Down by the river . . . carved on a rock . . . three little words . . . forget me not. There was something that carried the words along, like rowing a boat. And it was fun to say.

Now he felt better. Even if he still didn't know *precisely*

what a poem was, it was good to think he was getting *some* idea of it.

On Sunday afternoon Peter went for a walk around his neighbourhood. On a wall near a construction site he saw the words:

POST
NO
BILLS

Was that a poem?

He repeated. Post no bills. It wasn't much fun to say. And anyhow he didn't know what it meant. It sounded like something you shouldn't do.

On the wall of the corner grocery store, Peter saw this:

Could that be a poem?

Mmnn . . . well maybe.

Then Peter thought of his brother Bobby and the words that were written on his T-shirt:

When you're as
great as I
am it's hard
to be humble.

Surely that was no poem.

How about the menu in a restaurant?

SUNDAY SPECIAL

PLUMP, JUICY HAMBURGER
CRISP FRENCH FRIES
CREAMY MILK SHAKE (8 FLAVOURS)

95c

That sure sounded good to him. But was it really poetry?

On Sunday night after dinner Peter walked into the living room and sat down. His dad was sitting in a big easy chair reading the weekend newspaper.

From where he sat Peter could make out a story headline.

He wondered if headlines were poems.

"Dad," called Peter after a bit, "what's a poem, anyhow?"

Peter's dad peered over his newspaper.

"You know what a poem is, Peter," he said, rattling the pages of the newspaper and looking back in it.

"Wellll . . ." said Peter hesitating.

"You know the best way to find out," suggested Mr Todd, "is to look it up in the dictionary. It's time you started using it."

Peter went over to the family library and took the dictionary down from the bookcase. He looked for the letter "p" and found it. Finally, after a lot of searching and remembering his alphabet, he found the word.

> **poem**: *n*. 1. an arrangement of words in lines with a regularly repeated accent; composition in verse. 2. composition showing great beauty or nobility of language or thought. 3. a beautiful thing.

The first two definitions were puzzling to Peter. But the third, the one that said a poem was a beautiful thing made a little more sense. Still, it was confusing.

Peter went to bed that night feeling guilty. He still didn't know what a poem was and the English class was the first one on Monday morning. He was afraid Mr Howard, the English teacher, would be angry when he found out Peter hadn't managed to complete his homework.

The next day Mr Howard asked various members of the class to read their answers out loud. He first asked Liz Bolton what a poem was.

Liz, who always wore a nice ribbon in her hair, said a poem was like a beautiful shining lake at twilight.

Mr Howard nodded and thanked Liz. Next he asked Charlie Kucharik what a poem was.

Charlie Kucharik, who liked to put gum on your seat when you weren't looking, said a poem was fancy words recited by a guy with a squeaky voice.

The class laughed. But Mr Howard frowned. He then asked Pierre Caledonia.

Pierre Caledonia, who always came first in class, said a poem was whatever turned you on.

All during this time Peter was sitting as still as he could in his seat. He didn't want Mr Howard to notice him and ask him the question.

"Can you tell the class the definition of a poem . . . Marie Julien?" asked Mr Howard.

Marie Julien, who always had a ready answer for anything, said a poem was an expression of sublime love and beauty.

There was a bit of a hush after that. Marie had a way of putting things that took your breath away.

"Peter Todd," said Mr Howard, "can you tell the class in your own words the meaning of a poem?"

Peter's heart nearly stopped. Did Mr Howard really call his name?

"Peter, did you hear me?" said Mr Howard.

"Yes – yes sir," said Peter getting slowly up out of his seat.

"Well then," urged Mr Howard, "answer the question."

Peter hung his head. He didn't know what to say. The

only thing he could think of was *fudgsickle stick in the mud*. But he knew if he said that everyone would laugh at him. So at last he said:

"I don't know, sir."

Some of the people in the class snickered and giggled.

"Don't you have some idea?" prodded Mr Howard.

"No sir," said Peter, adding, "I tried to find out. I really did. I went round asking everybody. I even looked the word up in the dictionary. But I couldn't find the right answer. Everybody I asked had a different answer and nobody agreed. So I don't know. I'm sorry, sir, but I just don't know."

"I see," said Mr Howard evenly.

"So what is the *right* answer?" asked Marie Julien in a loud voice to Mr Howard. There was a long pause as Mr Howard stared into space. The boys and girls squirmed in their seats anxiously, and looked at each other across the aisles as they awaited Mr Howard's reply.

"Nobody really knows what a poem is exactly," began Mr Howard. "It's one of life's great mysteries.

"A poem," he added, "can be a song, a flying bird, the sunset. Or drops of water on your head.

"A poem," continued Mr Howard, "can be rhyming, like:

> A tisket, a tasket,
> A brown and yellow basket

Or free-verse:

> Lucy in the sky with diamonds"

Then Mr Howard took a piece of chalk and wrote on the blackboard:

The Sight
of
pumpkins and popsickles

or the smell of
green green grass
after you've mowed it

A Poem is : sand on your toe
soapsuds in your tub

All kinds of crazy wild things
The sound of cheese
Coke in your nose
Ice cream in your pie
Fudgsickle in the mud.

"FUDGSICKLE STICK IN THE MUD!" repeated Peter Todd at the top of his voice.

Mr Howard stopped talking suddenly and peered owlishly down at Peter. The rest of the kids turned around in their seats to look at him, and if looks meant anything, they looked like they thought Peter must have gone right off his nut! And Peter? Well Peter had a sheepish grin on his face and he was blushing as though he knew something nobody else did ....

From *Kites and Cartwheels*
by CLAUDE X. LA BRECQUE

Monday Morning

"Nerissa Jones, what *are* you thinking about? You're certainly not thinking about writing a story for me."

Miss Banks sat frowning away down that room like she'd left her contacts out. Sour as a green apple, she was.

"Raymond Smith's done a page already. What have you done?"

There wasn't no point in tellin' no lies. My bit of paper was as blank as that wall, and I didn't have no more idea of some "Exciting Adventure" than that desk lid.

"I'm thinking about my sister, Miss," I said.

"Well, there's a time and a place for everything," she comes back. "Now get your mind on your work, girl."

So I tried – but it's really hard, concentrating on story writing when your mind's all buzzing with other things. It's like a glass door inside your brain, I reckon. You can shut it hard as you like, but them other thoughts still keep showing through.

I could still see all their faces, and all the fussing and the clapping, and the smart, best turn-outs. I could see my sister in her bride-frock, looking like the queen of all the world. And my daddy's smiling mouth – and his crying eyes.

And looking down, like I did a million times Saturday, I could still see my pink silk shoes, shining when I danced.

And now I was sitting at my desk, looking this time at

those legs I'd had before, and the little white socks and old brown bumpers.

You don't stay special for long, do you? It don't seem five minutes before you're back to your old self again, doing sums and having to think up Exciting Adventures.

My Aunt Lizzie got there first, long before she was wanted in the house. My mammy shouted down the stairs, "You go sit a piece in the best room, look through them cards and presents."

But only Auntie Lizzie's Uncle Ben does what my mammy says. Auntie Lizzie's in the kitchen making tea and organising things before you know it.

But my daddy, he's good with her. Before she makes herself a nuisance he gets her laughing, tells her an old family joke he knows she likes; then he makes her feel important – which is only what she wants, I s'pose, being the oldest auntie of the bride. He sits her down and gets her checking the bills for the drink and the food, and the extra for the choir and the bells.

That's private family business, and she feels really good.

There's been talking for weeks about how my sister has her hair.

"No fussing," my mammy says, "just neat with a pretty ribbon there."

"You are joking, ain't you?" my sister says. And she threatens something *drastic* if she hears any more of that talk.

She has what she wants in the end: beautiful blown-out curls, looking like a flower in the moonlight. When I see

her coming down the stairs, I can't tell you how I feel. I want to smile till my face splits, and cry a bucket of tears, and there's this new feeling of no floor beneath my feet. And I can't breathe, too. I just stand there with my mouth open, making some funny noises or other.

And I think, Is this what happens, then? That girl in the next-door bed to mine – she leaves it in a heap every morning and grumbles in her sleep, and she never can find her shoes – does she come out like this, one day? Like a beautiful butterfly out of a tangly bush?

And then riding in that big car to the church. That's something special, with those pink ribbons fluttering like they're waving hello to people. You keep your eyes on your shoes, but you're really thinking, "It's me in here; and why can't my mates all be out in the street this Saturday morning?"

My mammy's with me; not crying. She's been too busy to think about what's really happening, I reckon. But I take a sideways look, and I wonder if she might be having a think back to *her* wedding day. Different to this, by the picture. Outside a little church in Kingston back home, where the sunny white walls made the whole world look brilliant and bright.

I s'pose she must have been thinking along the same lines, because she suddenly says, "Well, at least that old sun's putting on a show."

And I reckon he was. He made Clapham brighten up and smile. And my mammy sits back in her seat instead of perching nervous on the front; and she closes her eyes and mumbles something quiet.

So it's all going well according to the plans. I'm the happiest person in the world except my sister; Auntie Lizzie's gone in the first car; our car's running to time; and there's just my daddy and the beautiful bride waiting for the first driver to double back and get them.

Everything's perfect.

Except we turn round the corner up to the church and there isn't a living soul there.

"There ain't no wedding here today," the driver says, sliding back his glass. "This place is all shut up, missus, like the Lord's gone on holiday."

"That can't be the case," my mammy say. "Perhaps they've all gone in and shut the doors."

"Hey, you sure this is the right day?" the driver asks. "Give me a look of your invitation."

"I ain't got no invitation!" my mammy snaps. "I'm the mother of the bride. I don't get issued with no invitation. And what d'you think I am, stupid, not knowing the right day of my own daughter's wedding? And where's that first car gone?"

The driver shrugs his shoulders. "Search me. But there ain't no wedding here, that's for sure. I've never seen a place so closed up and empty."

I was getting real edgy with this driver now. He had the look on him that, all right, we were sitting in his car, and he did have to care a bit about our problem, but he wasn't going to move mountains for us.

"What's the name of this church you've brought us to?" I ask him, trying to put the baby back in his lap.

He gives me this long stare. It's a good job for him my

daddy ain't in this car, I'm thinking. He wouldn't be sitting there all don't-care if he was.

"Saint Thomas's," he says, resting his hands on the steering wheel. "That's the address your fellow gave us."

I come to, then. "Well, I can tell you that this ain't Saint Thomas's." I tell him. "I go to Sunday School at Saint Thomas's, and there's no way this is that place."

The driver said nothing, but he started pointing at the notice board, all slow and cocky.

THE CHURCH OF SAINT THOMAS, CLAPHAM COMMON, it said.

"Well, what are you doing, then?" I asked him, giving my mammy and me both a surprise. "Saint Thomas, Clapham *Junction* is what we want."

He didn't say no more. Just muttered a bit. But didn't he drive fast, now he knew it was his mistake! One pink ribbon came off, and the other was flapping and flying like a streamer. People had to jump out of the way just to save their skins. My mammy closed her eyes and knocked her hat on the tilt.

You should have heard the cheers when we got ourselves there.

The bride was waiting already and my daddy was walking in all directions at once. But did their faces start to smile!

Uncle Ben stopped it being a nasty turn-out with the car people.

"You gone the long way round buying peppers?" he says to my mammy. "You don't need to make such a big fuss of me."

And then it all went forward like the stories tell. I carried the bride's train and never tripped, and stepped up and back when the moments came. And everyone was happy. We sang, our families, like old Saint Thomas, Clapham Junction ain't never heard before. And back at home we sang and danced so hard, I never noticed I slept

.ny own in that bedroom till the next afternoon around .wo.

Now I can't get it out of my head, no matter what tricks I try. School Monday morning is all mixed up. I get the words of 'Once upon a time' down on that paper, but nothing else; and then Miss Banks is there, going on again.

"This just isn't good enough," she says. "Really, Nerissa Jones, haven't you got *any* ideas for an exciting story?"

From *I'm Trying to Tell You*
by BERNARD ASHLEY

The Wedding

I have been to a wedding
it was flowers and music and lace.
The bride was beautiful.
I knew her face
but the whiteness made her strange
and she didn't know me
though
I'm
her sister.

CHARLOTTE ZOLOTOV